Armed and Dangerous

Praying with Boldness

Jane L. Fryar

SAINT LOUIS

Library of Congress Cataloging-in-Publication Data

Fryar, Jane, 1950–

    Armed and dangerous : praying with boldness / Jane L. Fryar.

       p.   cm.

    ISBN 0-570-04997-0

    1. Prayer—Christianity.   I. Title.

    BV215.F78   1998

    248/3'2—dc21   97-25295

1 2 3 4 5 6 7 8 9 10   06 05 04 03 02 01 00 99 98 97

CONTENTS

PROLOG

....

EGRESS OR ACCESS?

The nineteenth century circus king, P. T. Barnum, traveled the United States amazing audiences with his showmanship. Each time the circus came to town, a tent would go up for the sideshow. The bearded lady. The sword-swallower. The fire eater. All were staples of Barnum's sideshows. And so were natural anomalies like two-headed calves and albino pigeons.

As visitors wandered through the tent, they eventually came to a sign with an arrow pointing toward "The Great Egress." As they followed the arrow, many expected to find yet another wonder. Instead they found themselves blinking in the sunlight. Those who hadn't known that *egress* and *exit* are synonyms did know then. Once Barnum had people's money, he didn't mind if they egressed.

Often in life we're more likely to be told how to egress than to receive free access to people or places of importance. As we think about coming to a holy God in prayer, the first question that should come to mind is this: Will we receive access or be given quick egress?

One of my favorite movies, *Sneakers*, revolves around a group of technical geniuses trying to gain access to a building with better security than the Pentagon. Most doors remain closed to anyone without a security card and a voiceprint on file with the building's computer. Coming to the door, employees say, "My voice is my passport." Recognizing the tone and pitches of a given voice, the computer releases the lock. It's a contemporary version of the "Open Sesame" cavern in which Ali Baba and his 40 thieves hid their loot.

When you and I pray, *our* voice is not our passport. *Our* word does not give us access. But Jesus' voice does. Jesus' word does. Jesus says, "In My cross, you are forgiven." Jesus' word says, "You have received right standing in heaven's throne room because of My death and resurrection." When we come to God, we come as His children. We come as brothers and sisters of the Lord Jesus. We can come boldly. We can expect, on the basis of God's promises, to receive access. What a wonderful privilege! What wonderful benefits! What a great God we serve!

As you read more about the access that belongs to you in Jesus, I pray that you will catch a bigger vision for how to use that access. I pray that you will see yourself as, yes, God's child, but also as a warrior in the army of light. I pray that you will realize more fully that God's Word arms you for the spiritual battles of your own life and for those battles we fight together as the Church Militant here on earth. You see, we *are* armed and dangerous to the forces of evil and of darkness.

In fact, in Jesus, you already now have victory over them. Stand firm in the faith, confident that your prayers are heard in heaven and that the gates of hell will never prevail against us.

1

ARMED AND DANGEROUS

Breathing anxious, shallow breaths, the woman made her way back to the courtroom. Her hands trembled in fear, and yet her fear pushed her forward. One more time. Maybe if she presented her case one more time, she would get a hearing.

All the neighbors encouraged her to forget it. After all, this judge held his appointment for life. Public opinion meant less than nothing to him. Not even divine opinion mattered. Nothing had moved him so far. Not her logic. Not her tears. Not her pleas for justice.

Even so, she shouldered her way through the crowd until she stood face to face with the only one who could make her life livable. The buzz of the proceedings in progress stopped. Silence hung in the air like a wet blanket on a cold night. The judge glared at the widow for a long minute. "You again!" he snapped. Then he sighed, shaking his head and curling his lip to form a sneer. She glared back. "Give me justice!" she demanded.

A few minutes later she walked away, her burden gone. The judge had done the right thing. Not for the right reason, but he had done the right thing. That was all that mattered to the widow. "Alright!" he had shouted in frustration. "I'll rule in your favor. Just stop pestering me! I'm sick of hearing it!" The widow thought about his words as she walked back down the dusty street toward home. She smiled.

Perhaps you recognize the thoroughly nasty judge and the determined widow as characters in a parable our Lord Jesus once told (Luke 18:1–8). Someone has called this story "The Widow's Might" (not to be confused with the incident known as "The Widow's Mite"). The meaning of our Savior's parable pivots on the contrast between the unjust judge and our loving, heavenly Father. If someone like this judge, someone so hard of heart and calloused in conscience, would give the widow what she needed simply because she kept asking for it, then how can we expect less from our heavenly Father? How can we sometimes fear that our Father, the one who gave His own Son into death for our sins, might disappoint us?

In fact, that's precisely the point our Lord Jesus drew out for His first hearers: "Hear what the unrighteous judge said; now shall not God bring about justice for His elect, who cry to Him day and night, and will He delay long over them? I tell you that He will bring about justice for them speedily" (Luke 18:6–8).

Think of it! You and I are "His chosen ones"! Through what our brother, Jesus Christ, did on His cross, we have now become God's own adopted children. God hears when those whom He has chosen cry out to Him. He acts on our behalf. He acts *speedily* Jesus says.

But then our Lord asks a pointed question: "When the Son of Man comes, will He find faith on the earth?" With this question, our Savior puts His index finger directly on one of the problems, perhaps the main problem, we face when we pray. What do we expect from God when we approach Him? How do we view Him? As heartless and unjust—like the judge who kept denying the widow relief? As someone whose idea of goodness, of help, of relief is a distorted parody? If so, that belief can keep us from trusting. And if in our heart of hearts we suspect His motives and doubt His love, how will we ever find the courage to throw ourselves on the mercy of His court? How will we ever pray in bold faith and persist in prayer in a way that honors God?

Come with Every Care

Throughout both the Old and New Testaments, our Savior-God coaxes, urges, invites, and even commands us to bring our needs to Him. He makes dozens and dozens of promises to hear and answer our prayers.

As you read a few of these invitations and promises now, think through what they reveal about God's character, God's heart.

> *Call upon Me in the day of trouble; I shall rescue you, and you will honor Me.* (Psalm 50:15)

> *It will also come to pass that before they call, I will answer; and while they are still speaking, I will hear.* (Isaiah 65:24)

> *Then you will call upon Me and come and pray to Me, and I will listen to you.* (Jeremiah 29:12)

> *Call to Me, and I will answer you, and I will tell you great and mighty things, which you do not know.* (Jeremiah 33:3)

> *Ask, and it shall be given to you; seek, and you shall find; knock, and it shall be opened to you.* (Matthew 7:7)

> *What man is there among you, when his son shall ask him for a loaf, will give him a stone? Or if he shall ask for a fish, he will not give him a snake, will he? If you then, being evil, know how to give good gifts to your children, how much more shall your Father who is in heaven give what is good to those who ask Him!* (Matthew 7:9–11)

> *[Jesus said,] "Whatever you ask in My name, that will I do, that the Father may be glorified in the Son. If you ask Me anything in My name, I will do it. ... Until now you have asked for nothing in My name; ask, and you*

will receive, that your joy may be made full. … In that day you will ask in My name, and I do not say to you that I will request the Father on your behalf; for the Father Himself loves you." (John 14:13–14; 16:24, 26–27)

Let us therefore draw near with confidence to the throne of grace, that we may receive mercy and may find grace to help in time of need. (Hebrews 4:16)

But if any of you lacks wisdom, let him ask of God, who gives to all men generously and without reproach, and it will be given to him. (James 1:5)

What truths do you see in these verses? Among other things, these promises prove that our God is no shriveled up Scrooge who peers down from heaven looking for ways to withhold His blessings and His help from us. Our God opens His heart and His hand to His children minute by minute, day by day, generation to generation. So generous are His promises, in fact, that they may sound too good to be true. And yet we know that God does not lie. He has proven Himself true to His Word time and time again.

The eighteenth-century hymn writer and preacher, John Newton, puts it this way:

> *Come, my soul, with every care,*
> *Jesus loves to answer prayer;*
> *He Himself bids you to pray,*
> *Therefore will not turn away.*

Jesus loves to answer prayer! What's more, He loves to enlist us, His people, no matter what our situation in life, in the holy work of prayer. Of course, God can work His will on earth even without our prayers. After all, our God is a powerful God, a loving God, and He delights in bringing hope, salvation, and deliverance to people. But He has in grace chosen to give us the privilege of partnership with Him in that work as we pray.

Because God hears and answers prayer, our prayers impact people's lives. The Bible gives example after example of individuals whose prayers transformed history, whose prayers mattered eternally. While Christians sometimes like to talk about "the power of prayer," we know that prayer in and of itself has zero power. The power released when we pray resides in the One who has invited us so often and so urgently to pray, the One whose death has given us access to the throne of the God of the universe—our Savior, Jesus Christ.

Armed? Dangerous?

Our Lord's invitation to pray and His promises to answer our prayers have armed us for spiritual battle. Whether we know it or not, whether we feel it or not, we are enemies to Satan and his army. They see us as dangerous, or potentially so. The demons know that our prayers are far more than sweet, pious thoughts. We are armed and dangerous in the spiritual battle that rages— invisible—all around us. Notice the way the apostle Paul links prayer with the stand believers take as members of Christ's army of light:

> *Finally, be strong in the Lord, and in the strength of His might. ... For our struggle is not against flesh and*

blood, but against the rulers, against the powers, against the world forces of this darkness, against the spiritual forces of wickedness in the heavenly places. Therefore, take up the full armor of God, that you may be able to resist in the evil day, and having done everything, to stand firm. Stand firm therefore, having girded your loins with truth, and having put on the breastplate of righteousness, and having shod your feet with the preparation of the gospel of peace; ... And take the helmet of salvation, and the sword of the Spirit, which is the word of God. **With all prayer and petition pray at all times in the Spirit, and with this in view, be on the alert with all perseverance and petition for all the saints, and pray on my behalf, that utterance may be given to me in the opening of my mouth, to make known with boldness the mystery of the gospel.** (Ephesians 6:10–19, emphasis added)

Jesus loves to answer prayer. Jesus equips us to pray bold prayers. Jesus uses our prayers to advance His kingdom. What an exciting privilege! What an awesome opportunity!

LOOKING AHEAD

As we approach the holy presence of our Lord in prayer, the words of the psalmist echo in our ears:

> *Enter His gates with thanksgiving,*
> *And His courts with praise.* (Psalm 100:4)

Praise provides a blessed starting place as we begin to pray. But what is praise? What does it accomplish? Why would God ask us to enter His presence praising and thanking Him? The next chapter will explore those questions.

Looking Inward and Upward

Think about these questions prayerfully. Talk with your prayer partner or with others in your prayer group about them if you can. See what you discover.

- Which of the Scripture promises you read in this chapter strike you as particularly encouraging? Explain.
- What past experiences or current situations have sometimes kept you from trusting that your heavenly Father would keep His promises, hear and answer your prayers?
- Based on your answers to the two questions above, what would you like to say to the Lord right now?

Practical Prayer Tip

If you find yourself drifting off to sleep while you pray, you need not feel guilty. What better place to fall asleep than in the arms of Jesus?! On the other hand, if you do want to stay awake, try walking around the room instead of sitting or lying down. Pacing also helps some people keep their minds from wandering while they pray.

2

THE SACRIFICE OF PRAISE

The message came shortly after midnight. At least that's what the cabinet officials, awakened by fists pounding on their front doors, would later recall. One by one, each of them pulled himself up out of the deep well of sleep into which he had mercifully fallen a few short hours earlier. High position had its privilege. But it also had its drawbacks. Among the worst was the truth that your life wasn't your own. The cabinet officials awakened that night to see this oft-repeated figure of speech coming literally true. Their lives were on the line.

The head of state whom they served had gained worldwide renown for his brilliant military strategies.

He and his armies had come out of nowhere to defeat a world power everyone had considered invincible. Science. Architecture. Literature. All thrived in his realm. On the other hand, so did fear. One wrong move and you forfeited your life. No questions asked. No appeals allowed. Rank didn't matter. Past service didn't matter. "What have you done for me lately?" That's the only question that counted.

Now, in the dead of night, one of this ruler's newest advisors made his way through the palace corridors on his way back to his own house. He had been able to buy some time. He awoke three of his friends—Hannaniah, Mishael, and Azariah—for, of all things, a few moments of prayer. No one strategized. The four friends had no time for it. Nor did they plan a way to get out of town. Instead, they approached the throne of God with an urgent request, a matter of life and death. What had King Nebuchadnezzar dreamed, and what did the dream mean? That's what they needed to know, and if they didn't find out, the sun would rise in the morning to shine on the dead bodies of all Babylon's highest ranking cabinet ministers and palace advisors.

Almost immediately, Daniel received a vision in response to the prayers of his friends. The vision told him all he needed to know to save his own life and the lives of dozens of others. He could have—and to our minds perhaps should have—rushed back to Nebuchadnezzar's throne room at once. But he didn't. He stopped to worship first. His prayer of praise included these words:

Let the name of God be blessed forever and ever,
For wisdom and power belong to Him.
And it is He who changes the times and the epochs;
He removes kings and establishes kings;
He gives wisdom to wise men,
And knowledge to men of understanding.
It is He who reveals the profound and hidden things;
He knows what is in the darkness,
And the light dwells with Him.
To Thee, O God of my fathers, I give thanks and praise,
For Thou hast given me wisdom and power;
Even now Thou hast made known to me what we
  requested of Thee,
For Thou hast made known to us the king's matter.
(Daniel 2:20–23)

If you or I received an appointment to one of our nation's highest offices at an early age—perhaps even in our teens—we might, as they say, be full of ourselves. Daniel indeed had the appointment, but not the arrogance. Daniel adored the Lord, the God of his fathers. Daniel was not full of himself; he was full of God's glory and grace. (See Daniel 2:1–49.)

How Big Is Your God?

The psalmist sometimes uses words like these, urging God's people to praise Him:

O magnify the Lord with me,
And let us exalt His name together. (Psalm 34:3)

In a strict sense, we cannot magnify God. We can't make Him any larger or any more gracious or powerful.

He already fills everything that exists (Jeremiah 23:24)! But as we rehearse God's majesty, His goodness and might, we grow in our comprehension of and appreciation for who He is and what He has done. Our picture of His goodness and glory is magnified.

We anchor our praises in what our Lord has revealed about Himself in His Word. Down through the centuries, Christians have incorporated words or phrases or whole chapters of the Bible into their prayers of praise. The prayer of Daniel you just read is one example of a Scripture portion that can and has been used in the prayers of praise God's people have offered to Him down through the ages. Praises fill the psalms. Other parts of Scripture as well show us what praise is and suggest ways to fill our own prayers of praise with truths about our majestic King.

Later on, the book of Daniel tells us, Nebuchadnezzar erected a golden statue that looked like himself. He then gave his people a choice: "Bow in worship to my statue or burn in agony in my fiery furnace." (See Daniel 3.) Centuries later the Roman Caesars demanded that all their subjects offer a pinch of incense to them in a show of loyalty. The rulers of ancient Egypt likewise insisted they be worshiped as gods. Monarchs in China and Japan down through the ages declared themselves to be deities and demanded the worship of their subjects. The egos of these rulers left them sleepless and out of sorts unless the praises of their people rang in their ears.

The true God, the God of the Bible, the Triune

God, does not need our praises. He is not some egomaniac who will be crushed if we fail to recognize His glory and goodness. Praising God doesn't change Him, but it works fantastic changes in *us*! As we magnify the Lord, as we exalt Him using the very words of praise He has given us for this purpose, His Word works in us an ever deeper realization that we serve an awesome God, a kind and wonderful God.

Daniel and his friends had every reason to fear for their lives when the king's agent knocked on Daniel's door at midnight. But when the four began to offer praise to the covenant God of Israel, their earthly nemesis—King Nebuchadnezzar—began to shrink in power and importance. Daniel's praises brought his earthly circumstances into a proper perspective. Nothing the puny Nebuchadnezzar could do would short-circuit God's love, God's wisdom, God's purposes for Daniel and his friends.

Imagine a six-year-old picked on by neighborhood bullies at the bus stop. Imagine the little boy's daddy hearing his son's cries through an open window. Imagine that daddy—a 6-foot, 5-inch defensive lineman for the Dallas Cowboys—bursting out the front door to his son's rescue. We may find ourselves feeling helpless, frustrated, and fearful as we face the problems in our lives too. But when we call out our Daddy's name, when we remember who He is and, especially, what He has done for us on our Savior's cross, Satan's threats and the damage he vows to inflict on us melt away like morning mist in the noonday sun.

Praise is the atmosphere of heaven. The psalmist identifies the Lord as the one "enthroned upon the praises of Israel" (Psalm 22:3). When we praise God, we invite Him to set up His throne here on earth, among His people. We enjoy being with Him, and we draw strength from His presence as He floods our minds and hearts with His Word of grace toward us in Jesus.

Praise—Our Weapon of Choice

God commissioned the tribe of Judah to lead the conquest of the Promised Land (Judges 1:1–9). The Lord's choice of Judah for this honor has several implications. Most important for us at this point in our discussion about prayer is the fact that Judah's name means "let Him [God] be praised." We read of several other instances in the Old Testament in which praise led God's people into battle, so to speak.

During the reign of King Jehoshaphat, for example, three nations joined forces in an effort to conquer God's covenant people. (See 2 Chronicles 20 for the details of this remarkable event.) Jehoshaphat gathered the people of Jerusalem for a public prayer service. He committed himself and his nation into the Lord's hands for safekeeping, praising God for who He is and for all He had promised and done in the past. When the king finished his prayer, a Levite named Jahaziel spoke. His prophecy included a complete battle plan directly from the Lord. On a human level, the "plan" must have seemed like not much of a plan at all. But it was God's plan—in two parts (2 Chronicles 20:15–21):

- **Part 1**—Don't be afraid, because the battle is Mine.
- **Part 2**—March out to the battlefield and find a good vantage point from which you can watch Me defeat your enemies. You won't need to fight at all.

When morning came, King Jehoshaphat followed God's instructions to the letter. In fact, the choir led the army out to the battlefield. As they marched, they led God's people in this "war chant": "Give thanks to the Lord, for His lovingkindness is everlasting." By the time Jehoshaphat and his warriors got to the battlefield, the fighting had already ended. Jehoshaphat and his soldiers had only to gather up the spoils—gold, jewelry, clothing, weapons. It took three days. In this case too, praise led the way to victory.

Praise is not a magical incantation. Rather, our praise serves as a Spirit-led reminder to ourselves that we serve a God who is both able and willing to help us, as the God who sent Jesus to die for our sins. As we face the challenges of our own life and service for Christ, Satan often tries to import the atmosphere of hell into our hearts. He wants to pollute our thoughts with fear or hatred or despair. These things are toxic to trust, to confidence in our Lord. Praises directed toward God, on the other hand, are toxic to Satan. When we begin to praise, God uses His Word of truth to clear from our minds the fear and lovelessness and hopelessness Satan works so hard to create in us. He hates to hear even the smallest, the weakest, the newest child of God begin to breathe prayers of praise heavenward. Praise thwarts the devil's plans for our lives.

A Sunday school class I once taught studied the account of Solomon's prayer on the day Israel dedicated the temple. The picture on the front of the leaflet showed King Solomon kneeling, his arms and face uplifted in praise toward heaven. One of my first-grade students studied the picture for a long while. Finally she said, "Oh, I get it! He's saying, 'Here I am, God! I'm Yours!'"

When we lift our hearts to the Lord in praise, that's what we're saying too. All in heaven—and in hell—take note of our words: "Here I am, God. I'm Yours."

LOOKING AHEAD

As we enter the presence of the holy God and as we begin to praise Him for His glory and goodness, we become aware of our own lack of goodness. Guilt, shame, and fear can begin to well up within us, making prayer uncomfortable. But our Lord has given us a way to remove those barriers so that He can draw us close to Himself. Chapter 3 outlines that process—confession and absolution.

LOOKING INWARD AND UPWARD

Think about these questions prayerfully. Talk with your prayer partner or with others in your prayer group about them, if you can do so comfortably. See what you discover together.

• Think about the statement "Praise is the atmosphere of heaven." What does it mean? What implications flow from this truth? Before you answer, read Revelation 19:1–6.

- Quite often the very times when we need most to remember our Lord's holiness, power, and kindness are the times when we feel least like praising Him. But praise is not a feeling. Think about a time when you didn't feel like praising God but began to do so anyway. What happened?

- What situations in your own life right now cause fear or lovelessness or hopelessness to well up in your heart? Get alone with your Lord and spend 10–15 minutes praising Him. Use the words of Psalm 145 as you meditate on God's goodness. Notice what happens to your worries and your anger as you magnify your Lord.

PRACTICAL PRAYER TIPS

If you do not already keep a prayer journal, start now. A small notebook will work well. On the first few pages, copy several prayers of praise from the Psalms. You may want to include one verse or a dozen from any given psalm. Simply select words you find meaningful. You may want to leave several subsequent pages blank. Use these for hymn stanzas, praise choruses, or more Scripture verses you find later that you would like to incorporate into your prayers.

3

C OALS FROM HEAVEN'S HIGH ALTAR

The day my eyes were opened. That's how I think of it, even now, decades later. Oh, I knew the official doctrine long before that day. My teachers had drilled and drilled. Holiness. My nation's whole system of religious ritual had come to stand on this foundation.

Yahweh alone was holy. When the holy met up with the unholy, the unholy would find itself immolated, incinerated, turned to ashes. Instantly. So went the theological theory. But while our teachers expounded on the taxonomy of holiness, my people descended ever deeper into a morass of violence, of materialism, of love-lessness. So went the everyday reality.

I can't recall exactly what occupied my mind earlier that day. It stopped mattering as I felt myself translated into the presence of Holiness Himself. I looked up. And at once I saw. I saw! Yahweh, the King of heaven and earth, on His throne. High. Exalted. I saw His glory, a glory that filled the heavens and the highest heaven. Seraphim attended Him—the "burning ones." The light of their holiness seared my eye lids. My ears roared with their words of praise:

> Holy, Holy, Holy, is the LORD of hosts, The whole earth is full of His glory.

The doctrines—so wooden, so sterile among my people—now scalded my heart. My sin. My people's sin. All of it lay like an open book before the holy God. "I am destroyed," I wailed. And I waited for the blow that would cast me into an eternal hell, away from the presence of Holiness.

It never came. Instead, one of the seraphs reached onto heaven's High Altar. I watched, speechless, as he took a tongs and removed a live coal. He flew to me and touched the coal to my lips. To purify. To consecrate. He said, "Behold, this has touched your lips; and your iniquity is taken away, and your sin is forgiven."

More came that day. A commission to serve. Words to speak. The promise of the Holy Seed—the Messiah whose blood would be poured out to purge sin forever. I saw it all, and I see it still. I—the "seer in Israel," Yahweh's prophet. *Would that all God's people were prophets!*

Sin. Grace. The truth can whiz over our heads like just so many lovely sounding theological words. Like Isaiah and his people of old, we probably have plenty of information. We have dissected the doctrines, memorized the definitions. We need, instead, to see. We need to see in a way that will transform our understanding of ourselves, of our world, of our desperate need for our Savior—the Savior whom God in His mercy has already provided.

What Do the "Seers" See?

Throughout the Old Testament era, God's people called the prophets "seers." These servants of the Most High saw beneath the surface of the ordinary, saw beyond the everydayness of human experience, saw into the heart of humans and into the heart of God. The seers saw the truth. Much of what they saw wasn't pretty. In fact, the truth Isaiah saw about himself filled him with terror. And rightly so.

When we pray, we enter the presence of the Almighty, the presence of Holiness. As we begin to praise our Lord for His majesty, His greatness, His wholly-otherness, we can find our hearts, too, filling with a deep sense of the uneasiness Isaiah experienced. The more clearly we see God for who He is, and the more clearly we see ourselves for who we are, the more conscious we become of the contrast. With Isaiah we are tempted to cry out, "I am destroyed!"

As long as sin remains for us an intellectual idea and holiness a theoretical ideal, the truth that we have sinned won't disturb us very much. But our sins are not just a set of demerits in God's book. We are not school children whose teacher adds a chalk mark behind the names of those who break a rule or two. No, sin is a malignant force at work in us, a malignancy we inherited from Adam and Eve. We help to perpetuate its damage as we disobey God's Law. We cannot tell where—or even if—its effects will end.

All of us every day add the spiritual equivalent of cyanide to the stew of human misery that poisons our planet. The effects of even our most secret sins cannot be kept to ourselves. Our gossip, our greed, our lust, our lovelessness—all these damage other people.

Our sins also damage us. By them we retard the Holy Spirit's transforming work in our lives. By them we impede His process of conforming us to the image of Christ (Romans 8:29). By them we diminish the degree to which we can represent our Savior in a world that needs Him so much. Every sin we commit and every good deed we fail to do thwarts our Lord's purposes for our lives.

Finally—and most important—our sins offend the Holy God. They break His heart. If you doubt this, read the book of Jeremiah. Or Hosea. Listen to our Lord plead with ancient Israel to return to Him. Hear as He compares their faithlessness to His covenant with adultery and as He characterizes Himself as Israel's hus-

band, rejected by her. Listen to the anger and pain in
His voice as He cries out:

> Listen to the word of the LORD, O sons of Israel,
> For the LORD has a case against the inhabitants of the land,
> Because there is no faithfulness or kindness
> Or knowledge of God in the land.
> There is swearing, deception, murder, stealing, and adultery.
> They employ violence,
>   so that bloodshed follows bloodshed. ...
> For a spirit of harlotry has led them astray,
> And they have played the harlot,
>   departing from their God. ...
> How can I give you up, O Ephraim?
> How can I surrender you, O Israel? ...
> My heart is turned over within Me,
> All My compassions are kindled.
> (Hosea 4:1–2,12; 11:8)

Our sins throw up roadblocks, barriers to genuine
prayer:

- Sins make us cringe, fearful in God's presence
  and eager to leave it. The Puritan preacher
  Jonathan Edwards wrote a now-famous sermon
  entitled, "Sinners in the Hands of an Angry God."
  Edwards' words portrayed God as a sadistic
  judge, dangling human beings by a thread over
  the fires of hell. Our sinful flesh, inflamed to terror by our disobedience to God's law, tries to convince us that Edwards' picture of God is true.
- The shame we feel because of our sins keeps
  us from communicating the needs of our
  hearts—our need for fellowship with our

Father, our need to praise Him for who He is and to thank Him for what He has done; our financial, relational, and medical needs; the needs of other people, people we care about. Adam and Eve hid in the garden, shamed by their sin. Shame like theirs is something like that of a jobless debtor who owes his banker a billion dollars—a sum larger than he could ever, ever hope to pay in 10 lifetimes. How could a debtor like that dare to ask his creditor for lunch money, let alone for an invitation to tonight's banquet or for a vacation cruise in the Bahamas? And how can we—we wonder—presume to enter God's presence to ask Him for anything when the I.O.U.s He already holds against us reach to high heaven?

The deeper the Holy Spirit leads us into His Word, the more clearly we see the contrast between our unholiness and the infinite holiness of our God. The more we grow in grace, the more seriously we will take our sins. But surprisingly, the more we grow in grace, the less alarmed we will be at our sins. Read those last two sentences again. Think them through: *The more we grow in grace, the more seriously we will take our sins. But, the more we grow in grace, the less alarmed we will be by our sins.* Why would that be?

Two Altars, One Reality

If we ever hope to approach a holy God to praise and worship Him, let alone to ask Him to help us or those we care about, the barriers posed by our sin must be demolished. It's at this point—at the point of shame and guilt and fear—that Isaiah's experience with his sins intersects our own. The same God who pulled down the barriers for Isaiah has also demolished them for us—in Jesus. Look carefully at what Isaiah wrote as he described this part of his vision:

> Then one of the seraphim flew to me, with a burning coal in his hand which he had taken from the altar with tongs. And he touched my mouth with it and said, "Behold, this has touched your lips; and your iniquity is taken away, and your sin is forgiven." (Isaiah 6:6–7)

The altar from which the seraph took the coal was not an earthly altar. This altar is the heavenly reality behind the earthly shadow or model that the Lord had commanded His people to construct in Jerusalem's temple. This is the high altar of heaven where the Lord Jesus offered His own blood for our sins, for all our sins:

> But when Christ appeared as a high priest of the good things to come, He entered through the greater and more perfect tabernacle, not made with hands, that is to say, not of this creation; and not through the blood of goats and calves, but through His own blood, He entered the holy place once for all, having obtained eternal redemption. (Hebrews 9:11–12)

Christ's blood, Christ's offering of Himself, has done away with our guilt once and for all. Like Isaiah, our iniquity is taken away and our sin forgiven. God goes to great lengths throughout all the Scriptures to convince us of that fact, to quiet our fears and to still our shame. Read, for instance, these verses—a few of the hundreds in Scripture that promise God's complete pardon for all our sins:

> Then the LORD passed by in front of [Moses] and pro-claimed, "The LORD, the LORD God, compassionate and gracious, slow to anger, and abounding in lovingkind-ness and truth; who keeps lovingkindness for thousands, who forgives iniquity, transgression and sin."
> (Exodus 34:6–7)

> I acknowledged my sin to Thee,
> And my iniquity I did not hide;
> I said, "I will confess my transgressions to the LORD";
> And Thou didst forgive the guilt of my sin. (Psalm 32:5)

> Thou didst forgive the iniquity of Thy people;
> Thou didst cover all their sin. (Psalm 85:2)

> For Thou, Lord, art good, and ready to forgive,
> And abundant in lovingkindness to all who call upon
>   Thee. (Psalm 86:5)

> He who conceals his transgressions will not prosper,
> But he who confesses and forsakes them will find com-passion. (Proverbs 28:13)

> I, even I, am the one who wipes out your transgressions
> for My own sake; And I will not remember your sins.
> (Isaiah 43:25)

> Let the wicked forsake his way,
> And the unrighteous man his thoughts;
> And let him return to the LORD,
> And He will have compassion on him;

And to our God,
For He will abundantly pardon. (Isaiah 55:7)

I will cleanse them from all their iniquity by which they have sinned against Me, and I will pardon all their iniquities by which they have sinned against Me, and by which they have transgressed against Me.
(Jeremiah 33:8)

Who is a God like Thee, who pardons iniquity
And passes over the rebellious act of the remnant of
  His possession?
He does not retain His anger forever,
Because He delights in unchanging love.
He will again have compassion on us;
He will tread our iniquities under foot.
Yes, Thou wilt cast all their sins
Into the depths of the sea. (Micah 7:18–19)

If we confess our sins, He is faithful and righteous to forgive us our sins and to cleanse us from all unrighteousness. (1 John 1:9)

[Christ] gave Himself for us, that He might redeem us from every lawless deed and purify for Himself a people for His own possession, zealous for good deeds.
(Titus 2:14)

Read those verses again; slow down as you do. Look for all the many ways the Holy Spirit pictures the fullness of His forgiveness: covering, cleansing, erasing, forgetting, pardoning, and so on. Our Savior-God not only sent Jesus to remove our sin, to take our punishment, He also works with diligence to convince us of that fact. He wants us to know it and to rely on it so that we have no fear or shame or guilt when we come into His presence.

Why Confess?

If all this is true (and it is), if God has already forgiven all our sins—past, present, and future—for Jesus' sake (and He has), then why bother to pray prayers of confession at all? What purpose does it serve? Why would we want to air our dirty laundry in the throne room of heaven? That's a good question. In fact, many sincere Christians have concluded that prayers of confession are unnecessary or even harmful! They may not say it in so many words, but their actions betray the belief that rests in their hearts.

Other Christians go on dutifully confessing their sins, day by day, or at least week by week in the public worship service, perhaps not understanding why they do it or what our heavenly Father intends that we gain by it. That, by the way, is the first truth we need to get clear. Our prayers of confession benefit God not one bit. He has given us the opportunity to pray prayers of confession to bless *us*, to do *us* good.

You see, God has lofty goals for us, a wonderful future in store for us. He wants nothing less than to recreate in each of us the image of His Son. He is in the process of transforming us into the image of Christ. We have already received Christ's righteousness—it was credited to our account when He died and rose again. Remember St. Paul's words?

[God the Father] made [Jesus] who knew no sin to be sin on our behalf, that we might become the righteousness of God in Him. (2 Corinthians 5:21)

That's a glorious truth. We're not fully experiencing this righteousness in our lives right now. Nor will we, as long as we live here on earth. But we are at this moment growing into our new identity as God's righteous people. In God's eyes we are righteous—fully. The seed of righteousness planted by God now forms the core of our being. And it has begun to grow bigger and stronger, replacing little by little our old ways of thinking and acting. Paul uses these words to describe that process:

*Now may the God of peace Himself sanctify you entirely; and may your spirit and soul and body be preserved complete, without blame at the coming of our Lord Jesus Christ. Faithful is He who calls you, and **He also will bring it to pass.*** (1 Thessalonians 5:23–24, emphasis added)

God does His cleansing work in us. He uses His Good News that in Jesus we have His total acceptance, His total pardon, His infinite love. None of these gifts depends at all on our performance. But knowing that we have them gives us the courage to come to Him with our failures in performance to receive from Him the strength we need to grow out of those failures. Note the two parts of His promise in 1 John 1:9:

*If we confess our sins, He is faithful and righteous to forgive us our sins **and** to cleanse us from all unrighteousness.* (emphasis added)

As we keep on confessing our sins—keep on saying what God says about them, He will keep on forgiving us. And He will keep on cleaning up the unrighteousness that remains in our lifestyle. What a fantastic promise! The seraph's coal assured Isaiah God had forgiven him and had cleansed his mouth so that Isaiah could speak for Him. Now, each time we confess our sins, God touches us with His Word, assuring us that He has forgiven us and that He is cleansing us so that we can live for Him. We can live with bold assurance that we are Christ's holy people; we can also pray with that same bold assurance.

LOOKING AHEAD

We may not feel such boldness as we approach God's throne. But we do not approach Him by ourselves. We have, by God's grace, a divine prayer partner—the Holy Spirit. Chapter 4 will explore the importance of the Spirit's partnership with us as we pray.

LOOKING INWARD AND UPWARD

As you talk with a friend or with others in your prayer group about the questions below, do so prayerfully. What can you learn from your own answers and from the answers of those with whom you talk?

- Think about Isaiah's experience, actually *seeing* the Holy God. How do you think you would have responded? Explain.
- When we confess our sins, we benefit by receiving God's assurance of forgiveness. We also bene

fit because with God's pardon comes His power to transform us more into the image of Christ. How is thinking about forgiveness in each of these ways especially meaningful for you?

- Based on the Scripture passages and other material you read in this chapter, what might you like to change as you think about your own prayers of confession?

PRACTICAL PRAYER TIP

Title a page or two in your prayer journal "Promises of Pardon." On those pages copy some of the Scripture passages from this chapter that you find especially powerful. Use another Bible translation if you will find that more personally meaningful. Then read God's promises before you begin to confess your sins each day. Remember, we can take our sins to God only because we already know—in Jesus—what His answer to our confession will be: Forgiven!

4

THE SPIRIT HELPS US IN OUR WEAKNESS

"If you don't have a will, make one." The message came just that bluntly. The young man who received it stood at the pinnacle of life. Purpose. Position. Power. He had it all, and more besides. But with one sentence he felt his life cut out from under him. We can easily imagine his knees buckling.

Where does a person turn at a time like that? Where do you go? What do you say? He turned away from doom's messenger to face the wall, to conceal the tears, to talk to the Lord. The enormity of the injustice welled up within him. His prayer wasn't much of a prayer. His words are never prayed from the chancel of any church today. He began this way: "Remember now, O LORD, ... how I have walked before You in truth and with a whole heart, and have done what is good in Your sight ..." His words trailed off, drowned by his tears. He couldn't finish his prayer. He didn't know what to ask.

Even so, heaven stirred. The young king continued to weep. But as he did, the Lord stopped His spokesman, Isaiah the prophet, turned him around, and sent him back to Jerusalem's palace with a revised message. "Go," God said, "say to Hezekiah, 'Thus says the LORD, the God of your father David, I have heard your prayer, I have seen your tears; behold I will add fifteen years to your life.' " But the good news did not stop there. "I will deliver you and this city from the hand of the king of Assyria; and I will defend this city."

What a story! What an answer to a prayer request that was never really spoken! Or was it? The text (Isaiah 38) clearly shows that Hezekiah didn't ask the Lord to save his life. But on the authority of Scripture we know that someone else took up Hezekiah's cause. Someone else prayed on his behalf. Read Romans 8:26–27:

> The Spirit also helps our weakness; for we do not know how to pray as we should, but the Spirit Himself intercedes for us with groanings too deep for words; and He who searches the hearts knows what the mind of the Spirit is, because He intercedes for the saints according to the will of God.

When Prayer Dissolves in Tears

Maybe you've found yourself, face to the wall, in a situation quite like that of Hezekiah. If so, you know what it's like to struggle to find the words to pray. We can stand speechless before God's throne for many different reasons. Sometimes we simply don't know what to ask God to do in a complex situation. Sometimes emotion overcomes us in the face of tragedy. Sometimes our need seems so big and our faith so small. No matter what the reason behind our weakness, we need never despair. We never pray alone. When we arrive at the throne of God, we can be sure the Holy Spirit drew us there and stands there beside us.

The night before our Lord Jesus died, He talked with His disciples about many important things, among them the power and position the Holy Spirit would soon assume in their lives. He connected the work of the Spirit with their prayers. As you read Jesus' words, notice the way His promises tie together:

> *Whatever you ask in My name, that will I do, that the Father may be glorified in the Son. If you ask Me anything in My name, I will do it. If you love Me, you will keep My commandments. And I will ask the Father, and He will give you another Helper, that He may be with you forever; that is the Spirit of truth, whom the world cannot receive, because it does not behold Him or know Him, but you know Him because He abides with you, and will be in you. (John 14:13–17)*

The Greek word Jesus used for "Helper" can be rendered literally "one called alongside." The Holy

Spirit has been called alongside us to help us pray ("whatever you ask in My name ...") and to obey ("you will keep My commandments"). Whenever we bring our needs or the needs of our world to our Father's attention, the Holy Spirit stands alongside us. Whenever we bring our sins and our need for growth in Christlikeness to heaven's throne, the Holy Spirit stands alongside us.

What does the Spirit do? He comforts, encourages, and strengthens us, to be sure. But His ministry to us is deeper still. Remember Romans 8? *The Spirit Himself intercedes for us with groanings too deep for words ...* The Holy Spirit stands alongside us as our spokesman. He's like a trusted family lawyer who speaks on our behalf, stating our case—no, *pleading* our case for us! That's why verse 28 can follow verse 27 with such certainty. The Spirit intercedes for us, and because He does ...

> ... we know that God causes all things to work together for good to those who love God, to those who are called according to His purpose.

To Impact Heaven ... and Earth

The truth of the Holy Spirit's intercession on our behalf goes a long way toward answering the question "Do my prayers change the outcome of things here on earth? Does prayer make a difference?" The answer is a resounding yes!

God's will toward us never changes, and that's a good thing. At a time in Old Testament history when the relationship between the Lord and His people had gotten about as low as it could go, God said this to His people through Malachi, His prophet:

> I, the LORD, do not change; therefore you, O sons of Jacob, are not consumed. (3:6)

God's changeless grace shields us too from the fallout that we by our sins have deserved. We are the "sons of Jacob" today—God's covenant people by faith in what our dear Lord Jesus has done for us in His suffering, death, and resurrection.

The Lord, in grace, had determined to take King Hezekiah to Himself in heaven. But as the king prayed and as the Holy Spirit interceded, God added grace to grace for Hezekiah. His will all along had been to maximize His grace to His servant. And through the prayers offered that day, God took the opportunity to do just that—granting Hezekiah 15 more earthly years, culminated by a joyful home-going when those years ended. Think of the apostle John's words:

> Of His fulness we have all received, and grace upon grace. (John 1:16)

Grace upon grace. Would Hezekiah have died 15 years earlier had he remained prayerless? We don't know. Perhaps the Lord would have raised up another intercessor, another prayer partner for the Holy Spirit. And if not, the king's death still would have been for him a transition to an eternity from which he would never, ever have wanted to return. Had Hezekiah died, would God's will have been thwarted? In a sense, yes. Perhaps that surprises you, but it need not; God's perfect will isn't always done here on earth. (If you doubt that, think back to your last sin.) Even if the Lord had not added that last, full measure of grace to Hezekiah's life, God had poured ample grace out on Hezekiah. In fact, He is still doing that in eternity. He—our Lord—does not change.

This adds a fantastic dynamic to the prayers we pray for ourselves and for others. As we intercede, prompted and led by the Holy Spirit, we share in His will and work. As He pours grace upon grace into human lives, we have a part in that! What a privilege! Actually, what grace!

One Last Question

The couple walked out of the hospital room leaning on each other. Eyes red. Faces puffy. The agony of the good-bye they had just said to their infant son etched on their hearts forever. In the chapel a few moments later the wife broke down. "We didn't pray hard enough," she sobbed.

What about that? Can we blame ourselves when the path of our lives plummets downhill? Or when others for whom we care are seemingly eaten alive by their circumstances? Can and does God act on people's behalf apart from our prayers as well as with them?

To answer that question, we must first recognize that no one prays with enough fervor, with enough consistency, with enough faith. That's why we need Jesus. His blood covers all our sins, even sins of prayerlessness. If we hear the Holy Spirit convicting us of a lack of zeal or commitment or faith in our prayers, we need to use God's remedy for sin—confession. When we confess, He is faithful to forgive us and to cleanse us from all unrighteousness (1 John 1:9). Second, we must recognize that God answers our prayers in ways He knows are the very best for us. Any given specific event may not *seem* best—or even good—at the time. But He is our Father. He will never abandon nor abuse His children. More about this in chapters 6 and 7.

The bottom line is this: God has such love for us that our sins can't stop His works of grace. God does not *need* our prayers. But *we* need to pray. We participate in God's work as we do that. He invites, urges, and commands us to pray. Even so, His kingdom *will* come, His will *will* be done in our lives with or without our prayers. But how poverty-stricken our souls remain if we fail to respond to God's invitation to bring our needs and the needs of others before Him.

The Holy Spirit is *your* prayer partner. He's ready—right now—to join His pleas with yours before the throne of grace. He wants to pour out grace upon grace in the lives of those you love and care about. What are you waiting for?

Looking Ahead

The Holy Spirit especially wants to partner with you in the work of bringing His kingdom of grace into the lives of those who don't yet know Christ. But how do we pray for the lost? How do we get beyond the petition "Dear God, bless the missionaries"? How is it that we march into the enemy's camp and "snatch some from the fire" (Jude 23)? How do we pray in a way dangerous to the kingdom of darkness? Chapter 5 explores those questions in depth.

LOOKING INWARD AND UPWARD

Talk with your prayer partner or with others in your prayer group about the questions below. Share the insights of Scripture with one another.

- In what ways does the Holy Spirit's role as your prayer partner make it possible for you to pray with boldness?
- The Spirit prays for you, and so does Jesus. Read Hebrews 4:14–16 and compare it with Romans 8:34. What requests do you suppose are made continually on your behalf?
- If you could call the Spirit of God alongside you right now to help you with a specific prayer-burden, what burden would you name? Why not do it?

PRACTICAL PRAYER TIP

Knowing that Jesus and the Holy Spirit both intercede for us can bring great comfort. Often it helps to have a human prayer partner too. Such a friend joins you in praying on a regular basis—daily, weekly, or monthly. You can share prayer lists, pray together on the telephone, or actually meet in person to pray. If you think this kind of support and accountability would be helpful and if you do not already have a friend like this, talk to the Lord about it. Ask Him to bring such a person into your life.

5

THY KINGDOM COME!

The believers prayed, and the earth shook beneath their feet. They were filled with the Holy Spirit and with the boldness for witness the Spirit brings.

Two of their company—Peter and John—had spent the night before in jail for an act of kindness, kindness done in Christ's name. The miracle of healing they had performed had attracted all kinds of attention. Several dozen, perhaps hundreds, had come to faith when they saw a 40-year-old who had never walked now doing cartwheels in the temple. But others who saw it and who heard the sermon that followed were not convinced. The majority who sat on Jerusalem's Ruling

Council, for instance. They heard themselves being implicated in the murder of Israel's Messiah, and they didn't like it. Not one bit.

Threats followed threats. Warnings piled on angry warnings. But in the end, no criminal charges would stick. Peter and John eventually found themselves outside the Council chamber, free to go. They hurried, unharmed, to the place where Christ's followers had gathered.

Together the group prayed—not for personal protection, not for relief from persecution, not for reassignment to a friendlier mission field. No, this was their prayer:

> O Lord, it is Thou who didst make the heaven and the earth and the sea, and all that is in them, … take note of their threats, and grant that Thy bond-servants may speak Thy word with all confidence, while Thou dost extend Thy hand to heal, and signs and wonders take place through the name of Thy holy servant Jesus. (Acts 4:24, 29–30)

Thy kingdom come. This petition lies at the core of the spiritual warfare to which our Lord has always called His people. This kind of bold witness has never made life "a flowery bed of ease," as the hymn writer once reminded us. The prayer prayed by the believers in Acts 4 quotes these verses from Psalm 2 about the challenges faithful witnesses of every era face:

> Why did the Gentiles rage, and the peoples devise futile things? The kings of the earth took their stand, and the

rulers were gathered together against the LORD *and against His Christ.* (Acts 4:25–26)

As the early Christians prayed, the nations did indeed rage and plot against the Lord and His Christ. The battle of the ages roared all around the people of God. It roars around us even now. But its outcome has never been in doubt. Elsewhere in Psalm 2, God the Father said to His Son:

Ask of Me, and I will surely give the nations as Thine inheritance,
And the very ends of the earth as Thy possession.
(Psalm 2:8)

After Jesus died and rose again to bring salvation to the ends of the earth, He told His followers:

All authority has been given to Me in heaven and on earth. Go therefore and make disciples of **all the nations***, baptizing them in the name of the Father and the Son and the Holy Spirit, teaching them to observe all that I commanded you; and lo, I am with you always, even to the end of the age.* (Matthew 28:18–20, emphasis added)

Do you see it? Like a baton relayed from one runner to the next in a race centuries long, the kingdom of God passes from one generation to the next, from one nation to the next. Jesus *did* ask the Father to give Him the nations. In response to that prayer, the Father did just that, and in doing so made Jesus' life and death the essential part of the answer. Then Jesus passed His authority, His message, His Word on to His disciples, and through them to faithful witnesses down through time's corridor, so that now the Good News has come to us also.

What's more, through Jesus, the Father says to us, "Ask of Me, and I will give *you* the nations." When we pray "Thy kingdom come," we join the Holy Trinity in the work of bringing the kingdom of Christ to a dying world. Our Lord uses our prayers as an essential part of fulfilling His promise, the promise He made to His Son before time began. We ask—invited and commanded to do so by God Himself. And God continues to work in the hearts of human beings through faithful witnesses to His Gospel.

What "Kingdom"?

Relatively few people live under kings in our world today. The kings we know serve mostly as figureheads, as symbols of empires from an earlier era, an era before modern republics and parliamentary democracies. And yet we live in a world caught up in what we might call "the clash of two kingdoms." Whether or not any given individual realizes it, each of us belongs to one side or the other. Each of us holds citizenship in one kingdom or the other. No human being can claim neutrality in this war.

On one side stand the prince of darkness, his demons, and his human victims; on the other, the Prince of Light, the holy angels, and Christ's human servants. While some adherents of Christianity reject the military symbolism of Scripture and of many historic

Christian hymns, the Bible leaves no doubt that our warfare is real and that the outcome matters. Whoever is not "with Christ" is "against Him," whoever does not "gather" souls for His kingdom, "scatters" and, in scattering, serves the darkness. (See Matthew 12:30.)

In the early years of her history, Israel had not yet designated a capital city. Saul, Israel's first king, set up camp at various places around his people's territory. Wherever the king camped, there the capital stood. In a similar way, the kingdom of Christ today is a nongeographical kingdom. Wherever our King Jesus sets up His camp in human hearts, there the kingdom has come. When we pray for the coming of Christ's kingdom, we ask the Spirit of God to do His holy work in people to convert their allegiance from darkness to light, from death to life.

As the kingdom of Christ comes to individuals, the Spirit continues His work, gathering those individuals together around His Word. Our King Jesus camps, as it were, among us when we gather as His church to worship Him and to encourage one another in the faith we share. The church serves as a sign, an emblem, a banner of the kingdom of Light that has already come here on earth.

One day—very soon—the Lord Jesus will return visibly to earth with the army of heaven to gather His army on earth to Himself. He will take us to heaven where we will celebrate forever the victory the Lord of glory has won for us over the hosts of darkness and death by the blood He shed on His cross. When we pray

"Thy kingdom come," we ask our Lord not only to preserve and extend His church, but we also ask Him to return with the angel army of heaven to put an end to the conflict that rages here on earth and to take all His scattered, embattled children home.

The Dark Side

For more than 20 years now, our culture has been shaped by the *Star Wars* phenomena. When George Lucas planned the first film in his trilogy, no one could have guessed the impact it would make, the merchandise it would sell, or how long it would last. But the struggle between good and evil, light and darkness, is classic. In *Star Wars* art mirrors life. Until the last scene plays itself out, the outcome of the struggle lies in doubt. The drama continues right to the very end.

The *Star Wars* films picture the philosophy of dualism at its finest. Dualism rivals Christianity in worldwide acceptance, and possibly even bests the Christian faith in sheer numbers of adherents. Whether they consider themselves dualists or not, most of the world's people live in doubt about life's outcome. Will evil or good prevail? Will darkness or light prove stronger in the end? In dualistic thought, the two forces lie locked in perpetual battle. Dualists believe the battle will last forever, that neither side will ever or *can* ever defeat the other.

Christians reject such a bleak view. A song popular in Christian circles a few years ago included this refrain: "I've read the back of the Book, and we win!" In fact, in

Jesus' open Easter tomb the victory is ours already. The outcome of life's battle has never been in doubt. Light scatters darkness—always. Holiness defeats evil—always.

But that's not always what we see as we pick up the morning newspaper, is it? We know from our own experience that the darkness does not lie still, waiting for someone to find and follow it. No, spiritual darkness is ...

- *Active*—[Jesus said,] "For a little while longer the light is among you. Walk while you have the light, *that darkness may not overtake you*; he who walks in the darkness does not know where he goes" (John 12:35, emphasis added).
- *Powerful and enslaving*—[Paul writes,] "For He delivered us from *the domain of darkness*, and transferred us to the kingdom of His beloved Son" (Colossians 1:13, emphasis added).
- *Limited by the power of the light Christ brings*—[John writes,] "*The darkness is passing away*, and the true light is already shining" (1 John 2:8, emphasis added).

We dare not underestimate the power of darkness. Peter did that and ended up denying Christ. Judas toyed with the darkness, and it stole his soul. On the other hand, we dare not despair. Our Lord does not want us to adopt a "hunker down in the bunker" mentality. The church of Jesus Christ is on the march, not under siege, no matter how His people may sometimes act. Our Commander promised this about the rock-solid truth of His Gospel:

Upon this rock I will build My church; and the gates of Hades shall not overpower it. (Matthew 16:18)

Hell does not advance on us. No, Satan and his demons are the ones fighting a holding action. God has, by our Savior's victory on Calvary, pushed the darkness back; as we continue to unite in prayer against it, we keep on pushing it back. We may indeed sow the seed of the Gospel in tears, as did the early Christians, but we need have no doubt that we will reap a harvest of joy—just as Psalm 126 promises.

The Hardest Prayers to Pray

Maybe you've had a son or nephew who joined the wrestling team at school. Maybe you've noticed that as the wrestlers grow more skilled, the matches grow more difficult to watch. The more skilled the opponents, the more painful the matches. In fact, the Greek word for such a struggle is the word from which we get the English word *agony*. The apostle Paul used just this word for struggle as he described his own wrestling in prayer:

For I want you to know how great a struggle [or agony] I have on your behalf, and for those who are at Laodicea, and for all those who have not personally seen my face, that their hearts may be encouraged, having been knit together in love, and attaining to all the wealth that comes from the full assurance of understanding, resulting in a true knowledge of God's mystery, that is, Christ Himself, in whom are hidden all the treasures of wisdom and knowledge. (Colossians 2:1–3)

Paul agonized in prayer that the Gospel would continue to grow in the hearts of these believers, that they would grow up in the love of Christ, and that they would not be led away from the precious truth they had trusted. Satan opposes no prayer so much as these kinds of prayers. When we pray "Thy kingdom come," we come up against the full forces of hell. Asking the Father to give us the nations is a struggle; sometimes even agony.

Praying for the lost, interceding for missionaries and other Christian witnesses, grappling in prayer for new believers that God would sustain in them a vibrant and growing faith—these prayers are not easily prayed, though they may look that way from the outside. When we pray such prayers, we stand armed—with the Word and promises of God—and dangerous—deadly, really—to the dark powers that oppose God and His Christ. By the grace of our Lord we join Peter, John, and the army of all other Christians down through the ages who have prayed—not for relief from persecution, not for reassignment to a friendlier mission field, not even so much for personal protection, but for this:

[Lord,] grant that Thy bond-servants may speak Thy word with all confidence, while Thou dost extend Thy hand to heal. (Acts 4:29–30)

The nations need that healing. Individuals whom we know by name need that healing. When we pray for it, we pray confident of God's promise: "Ask of Me, and I will surely give the nations as Thine inheritance, And the very ends of the earth as Thy possession" (Psalm 2:8).

Looking Ahead

God's Word invites and encourages us to pray for the lost. It also encourages us to ask for other things, for things that we—and others—need. One promise connected with this comes from 1 John 5:14–15:

> *This is the confidence which we have before Him, that, if we ask anything according to His will, He hears us. And if we know that He hears us in whatever we ask, we know that we have the requests which we have asked from Him.*

But what *is* the "will of God" and how do we know how to pray "according to it"? Chapters 6 and 7 will explore those questions as God works through His Word to build the bold confidence the apostle John wrote about.

Looking Inward and Upward

Talk with people in your prayer group or with at least one other Christian about these questions. Share your insights with one another.

- What experiences have you had in praying for those without Christ and for those who work to bring the Gospel to people who have never heard it?
- Chapter 4 talked about the help God's Spirit provides when we pray. How is knowing that the Holy Spirit prays with you a help when you pray for God's kingdom to come into the lives of individuals or groups of people ("the nations")?

- Often we fail to pray in specific ways simply because we lack information about how God is bringing His kingdom to the nations. Most often He does this through people. How could you find out more about specific Gospel outreach efforts so that you can pray more intelligently?
- In Matthew 9:38, Jesus asks His disciples to pray for workers in His harvest fields. In the very next verse (10:1), Jesus sends them out to share the Gospel. They became part of the answer to their own prayers! Has that ever happened to you? How do you react to that possibility?
- Based on this chapter, what changes would you like to ask God, by His grace, to work in your heart regarding His coming kingdom? Why not pray those prayers with your prayer partner or prayer group now?

PRACTICAL PRAYER TIP

Events in the world around us do not happen apart from the "clash of the kingdoms" you read about in this chapter. In fact, this clash and the unseen spiritual battles that rage around us all the time can and often do *cause* the events we hear about on the six o'clock news. Try this for a week: Watch the news or read the newspaper with a pad and pen in hand. Ask God to show you what and how to pray for specific situations so that His kingdom would advance. Jot these insights in your prayer journal on a page headed "Thy Kingdom Come!"

6

PRAYING IN THE WILL OF GOD

The nervous little clutch of men made their way through the night. A full moon scattered light on the trees; nonetheless, the darkness draped their mood like a shroud. Down a dusty street they walked in silence, out one of the city gates, and on to the base of a hill where a grove of olive trees stood. The leaves rustled, stirred by the breeze. Then the group's leader broke the silence. "Stay here," He said. He motioned for three of those closest to Him to follow as He walked away.

The word Gethsemane *means "olive press." A painful irony. The full pressure of hell's power was about to crush the gentle soul of Jesus. He fell on His face a few yards away from Peter, James, and John as the horror of hell welled up in His heart. He saw the army of Satan rising to stand opposite Him on the plain of eternity. He began to struggle in prayer. "Father, if it is possible, let this cup pass from Me; yet not as I will, but as Thou wilt."*

He lay still, chilled by His knowledge of what had already begun. Later, when He forced Himself onto His feet, He found His friends asleep, numbed by grief. He woke them with a question: "Could you not watch with Me? Not even for an hour?" He added a command, an urgent request: "Watch and pray. Stand your ground in prayer or you will surely fall into the enemy's temptations."

He walked away, crumpled to the ground, and began to agonize in prayer a second time: "My Father, if this cannot pass away unless I drink it, Your will be done." Cold sweat poured off His face. It soaked His clothes as the battle continued. The Savior's friends dropped off into sleep again, worn out by the sorrows of the day. Jesus saw. He repeated His prayer. The stars twinkled in a silent heaven as the betrayer made his way in the darkness toward the garden.

You know the rest of the story. The series of farces that passed as legal proceedings. The stumbling walk toward Golgotha. The darkness and death. The shout of triumph: It is finished! Seven centuries earlier, the prophet Isaiah had written about the outcome of our Lord's ordeal:

> As a result of the anguish of His soul,
> He will see it and be satisfied;

By His knowledge the Righteous One,
My Servant, will justify the many,
As He will bear their iniquities. (53:11)

God was satisfied. The price of redemption had been paid in full. Satan's hostages could go free. But what about the prayers of Gethsemane? Did the heavenly Father answer Jesus? Or, did He refuse to consider His own Son's requests? And if He did, what does that say to *us* about our chances of getting a hearing in heaven's court?

Thy Will Be Done?

You probably recognize the subtitle of this section as coming from the model prayer Jesus taught His followers. Sometimes called "The Disciples' Prayer" (in contrast with "The Lord's Prayer," the prayer Jesus Himself prayed the night before He died—John 17), the familiar words have fallen from the lips of Christians down through the ages. We have prayed and studied and marveled at the words. The petition about God's will has both comforted and confounded saints since Jesus first introduced it.

For a full 20 years in my own life, I refused to repeat this petition. I felt condemned and rebellious when I fell silent as the believers around me prayed it. But I felt hypocritical and inauthentic when I joined in. My problem lay much deeper than the words themselves. Looking back now, I recognize that I was wrestling with a question common to many Christians. Simply put, it goes like this: *Can God and His will be trusted?* Until we answer that question—personally—with a firm *yes*, asking our Lord to help us or to supply what we need is impossible.

How can someone ask God for a more rewarding job if he suspects the Almighty may want him to remain miserable and poor? How can someone ask God to mend her marriage if she thinks God may want to punish her for her sins by putting her through a divorce? How can someone ask God to heal a friend's cancer if both people believe God may have sent the disease? I could not pray "Thy will be done" and mean it because my picture of God was too distorted. If your picture of God is flawed, your prayers will be too.

For a while, in the depths of that time of despair, I knew for sure only that God would forgive my sins and take me home to heaven when I died. For the rest—my own troubles and the needs of the people I loved—I felt that all of us were pretty much on our own. I had picked up a view of prayer that amounted to little more than, as Lucy of *Peanuts* fame would say, "hoping to goodness." But even Charlie Brown recognizes that "hoping to goodness is not theologically sound."

Many Christians tack the phrase "Thy will be done" onto every prayer they pray. It serves them as a kind of "divine loophole." If things don't work out, no one can blame the pray-er. God has simply enforced "His will" instead of doing what we have asked. Mark Twain once heard a preacher trying to explain God's will. Twain complained that the explanation was so confusing that "the oldest man in the world couldn't figure it out." When we, with our finite minds, try to cover up our lack of faith or our limited understanding by spreading a blanket labeled "God's Will" over it, we can quickly find ourselves sprawling in a deep ditch of doubt. Maybe you've lain there a time or two. I know I have.

Or, maybe you've found yourself in the ditch on the opposite side of the fence. Those who've fallen into it picture prayer as a kind of "twist-God's-arm-hard-enough-and-long-enough" proposition. Believe hard enough and long enough, according to this theory, and you can command God to do anything. Yes, they do mean to say *command*. This theory is taught just this way in some so-called "faith-word" circles. When things don't work out, when the sick person dies or the bankruptcy goes through, no one can blame God. Instead, blame falls on the victim. The patient didn't have enough faith. The out-of-work friend wouldn't buckle down in prayer or didn't march around the house shouting the right words loudly enough. That's a deep ditch too. I know. I've lain there as well.

Can you see that Satan uses the backhoe of unbelief and fear to dig *both* these ditches? The person who uses the words "Thy will be done" may truly trust God's will—just as our Lord Jesus in Gethsemane did. On the other hand, such a person may have no true confidence at all that God will hear and help. The person who demands at the top of her lungs that God do what she bids Him do based on her own "faith" may be merely misguided. Or, she may shudder at the thought of turning her situation over to the Lord in its totality, allowing Him to do the best things for her; the thought of "His best" may scare her silly.

Dear God, Can I Trust You?

I rescued my puppy, Marty, from the county dog pound the day he was to be euthanized. I have no certain knowledge about his past, but his behavior seems to say he's had a tough life. One day he lay in his favorite spot at the top of the stairs. From there he can see out a window to the street; he plays sentry, warning me about the school bus and the *Schwann's* delivery truck. On that particular day, though, he's the one who needed protection. He saw something—I don't know what—out that window and began to quiver with fear. When I noticed him trembling, I tried to pick him up. He wouldn't let me. He squeezed behind the sofa to tremble there. His panic lasted for well over an hour, but he wouldn't come close enough so I could comfort him.

As I sat nearby feeling helpless, I began to think about the pain our Lord must sometimes feel when trust comes hard for us. Trusting God runs contrary to our sinful nature. Maybe you can think of times in your life when you needed your Lord's comfort, the reassurance of His presence and His power. But perhaps the more your panic grew, the deeper you burrowed into yourself. The bigger our fear, the harder it sometimes becomes to run to God for help. So what is the truth? *Is* God trustworthy?

We usually consider the people in our lives trustworthy if they do what they say they will do. Those who keep their word earn a reputation for trustworthiness. If that's the definition, then our Lord truly deserves the title. He has never reneged on a single promise. Remember the words of the apostle Paul:

> *He who did not spare His own Son, but delivered Him up for us all, how will He not also with Him freely give us all things?* (Romans 8:32)

When God gave Jesus to die for you, He proved Himself trustworthy. The will of God to which Jesus Christ assented in the Garden of Gethsemane centered on our eternal good, our eternal life. Because God wanted from all eternity to give us this gift of everlasting life, Jesus came and died. God's love for you lies at the very heart and core of His will. That's why when you or someone you know needs God's help, you don't have to fret about **any** of these questions. You can cross them off your list—and I do mean *cross* them off. In the cross of Jesus you need no longer ask

- Do I have enough faith to pray for this?
- Does God love me enough to do this for me?
- Do I deserve to ask this?
- Do I dare ask for something so big?
- Should I bother God with something so little?
- Is this request "spiritual enough" and "unselfish enough"?
- Does God care about this?

Instead of asking those kinds of questions, you can remind yourself of two key truths:

- God let His Son die on the cross for my sins and for the sins of everyone in the world.
- Since God already gave His best, He will not withhold the rest.

God delivered once and for all on the dozens and dozens of promises He had made about sending His Son. The day Jesus died on Calvary, God proved Himself trustworthy. Because He has shown such great love for each one of us, we can—in confidence—bring all our other concerns to Him as well.

Suppose a millionaire adopted an orphan from an impoverished third-world country. Suppose he arranged for her to become a citizen of his own nation. Suppose he provided her with the best food, rooms and rooms of toys, her own swimming pool, and a bedroom fit for a princess. Suppose he set up a trust fund to pay for her education, even for a Ph.D. if she wanted it. Suppose he showered her with affection and spent endless hours thinking about how to increase her sense of safety and contentment.

Now suppose one night she awoke with a stomach ache. Would a benefactor like this want her to keep her pain to herself? Of course not! Suppose she came home from school one day hungry. Would a father like this want her to hesitate to ask for cookies and milk? Of course not! Suppose he told her he was concerned about other orphans who might be hurt and harassed. Would she hesitate in asking him to help her friends back in the orphanage? Surely not!

And neither does our heavenly Father want us to hesitate to bring our every need and concern to Him. He gave His only Son into death for us. He *wants* the best for us, and He *will do* the very best things for us and for those whom we bring to Him in prayer. For all the years I knew her, my grandmother had a plaque on her bedroom wall that read something like this:

> God knows. He loves. He cares.
> This truth no fear can dim.
> He always does the best for those
> Who leave their needs with Him.

This is all true, but it can seem trite, especially when we find ourselves mired in the swamp of adversity. When we're hip-deep in alligators, discouragement and fear can threaten to drown us. Satan, who never fights fair, will assault us at just the wrong time every time with his lies and innuendos. "Is God *really* good?" he will ask. "Are you *sure* you can trust what He has said?"

We cannot fight fear and disappointment, panic, doubt, and discouragement on our own. But we're not on our own. Remember the Paraclete—the one called alongside to help us in our weakness? The one who "intercedes for the saints *according to the will of God*"? (Romans 8:27, emphasis added.) The Holy Spirit continually prays for us; He is praying for *you* right now! Think of it! Knowing that fortifies us for the fight. He's the one who creates our faith in the first place; He's the one who must sustain it.

We need not drown in doubt. We need not struggle to remake ourselves into the image of some kind of spiritual supermen or wonderwomen. We need not grope around in the murky waters of our circumstances trying to find our own spiritual bootstraps so that we can yank ourselves out of the swamp and away from the jaws of the alligators. Instead, we can call out to Christ. We can confess our weakness and ask for His strength. We can keep looking to His Word of truth. We can trust Him to work through that Word even when, at the time, it seems as dry as sawdust.

Regardless of how we feel, regardless of how little enthusiasm we can manage to muster up in our prayers, Joseph's garden tomb was empty on Easter morning. God has kept His word about that. Jesus Christ did die—and rise again. And He will keep His every other promise too. So then as we pray, we focus on God and His Word, not on where our feelings fall along the faith/doubt continuum. We pray God's revealed Word—His promises—with total confidence that His Word is indeed His will.

The Will of God

It will help you grow in faith for prayer if you read the Scriptures for yourself with an eye toward mining the diamonds of promise you will find there. Here are a few I find especially meaningful as I pray God's will into my own life and into the lives of other people:

> But the path of the righteous is like the light of dawn,
> That shines brighter and brighter until the full day.
> (Proverbs 4:18)

He gives strength to the weary,
And to him who lacks might He increases power.
Though youths grow weary and tired,
And vigorous young men stumble badly,
Yet those who wait for the LORD
Will gain new strength;
They will mount up with wings like eagles,
They will run and not get tired,
They will walk and not become weary.
(Isaiah 40:29–31)

"No weapon that is formed against you shall prosper;
And every tongue that accuses
   you in judgment you will condemn.
This is the heritage of the servants of the LORD,
And their vindication is from Me," declares the LORD.
(Isaiah 54:17)

Those who hopefully wait for Me will not be put to shame. (Isaiah 49:23)

"My people shall be satisfied with My goodness," declares the LORD. (Jeremiah 31:14)

The joy of the LORD is your strength.
(Nehemiah 8:10)

[Jesus said,] "For this is the will of My Father, that everyone who beholds the Son and believes in Him, may have eternal life; and I Myself will raise him up on the last day." (John 6:40)

The peace of God, which surpasses all comprehension, shall guard your hearts and your minds in Christ Jesus. (Philippians 4:7)

My God shall supply all your needs according to His riches in glory in Christ Jesus. (Philippians 4:19)

Beloved, now we are children of God, and it has not appeared as yet what we shall be. We know that, when He appears, we shall be like Him, because we shall see Him just as He is. (1 John 3:2)

LOOKING AHEAD

Much of the asking we do—for ourselves and for others—in prayer turns around three kinds of concerns. We pray for physical healing, for help with financial need, and for the resolution of family problems. God's will for us in Jesus is always and fully good. But what—exactly—can we expect when we bring specific requests for health, wealth, and family happiness before God's throne? Chapter 7 probes that question.

LOOKING INWARD AND UPWARD

Share your thoughts about some of the questions below with someone you trust. You may be surprised—and encouraged—to find how much you and that person have in common.

- Which paragraph(s) in this chapter most challenged, comforted, or provoked you? Explain.
- To what Scriptures do you personally turn when you need to be assured that you can count on God's trustworthiness?
- Choose one of the Scripture verses on pp. 72–74 and think about how you could incorpo-

rate it into a prayer appropriate for yourself or someone you know. Let your partner or the members of your group do the same. Then pray your prayers out loud, one at a time. (If you feel more comfortable, jot down key phrases you want to include before you begin praying.)

PRACTICAL PRAYER TIP

Praying with someone else or with a group can feel intimidating at first. You may feel more comfortable if you make format decisions before you begin to pray. For example:

- You may want to hold hands as you pray. When the person who begins praying finishes, he or she can squeeze the hand of the next person. The last person to pray can add an amen when he or she is done speaking.
- Don't panic if the person praying falls silent for a few moments. Give that person time to collect his or her thoughts before going on.
- It doesn't matter if two (or more) people pray for the same thing; each person will probably approach it from a different angle.
- You may want to write each prayer request on a separate note card. Deal out the cards as you begin. That way everyone has at least one thing to pray about and you won't leave anything out.

7

NEEDS, NEEDS, AND MORE NEEDS

"Your friend is ill." That was all the message said. No elaboration. No emotion. Not even a request. The two sisters who sent it counted on the fact that Jesus would know what to do. He did. He took 48 hours to tie up loose ends and to let events unfold just far enough. Then He and the Twelve headed out—on foot—for Bethany.

They arrived late. No one knows what Mary and Martha thought of the fact that Jesus got there four days after the funeral. (I know what I would think.) Perhaps we get an inkling in Martha's first words to Jesus: "Lord,

*if You had been here, my brother would not have died."
Later, in the cemetery, Mary repeated Martha's words.
She quoted them exactly: "Lord, if You had been here
…." No doubt the sisters had been talking, puzzling over
His absence, questioning His delay. They believed Jesus
was their friend. They had even begun to see Him as
their Messiah. But this …*

*This turn of events must have dredged up every
doubt and exposed every fear that lies buried in the
darkness of human hearts. Where is God when we hurt?
Why is He so slow to help? Doesn't He know? Doesn't
He care? But despite their confusion, in the face of their
fear, God was about to act.*

*Their miracle began with a command: "Open the
tomb," Jesus said. His words were too much for Martha
after everything that had happened, everything that
had gone wrong. She blurted out a blunt truth: "Lord,
by this time the corpse will stink! He's been dead four
days." She was right, of course. When the stone was
rolled up the rocky channel that held it in place, everyone knew Lazarus was truly dead.*

*The second command must have shocked Jesus' lis-
teners even more, but then they weren't the ones who
would obey it: "Lazarus, come forth!" And he did. The
creature responded to the voice of the Creator. Like little
children on Christmas morning, Lazarus' friends
unwrapped the gift—God's gift. As they untied the grave
clothes, they caught a glimpse of the truth: Jesus' miracle
was no cheap sideshow sleight-of-hand. Jesus had peeled
death's bony fingers off the throat of one of its victims.*

It was a sign of things to come.

I can never read John 11 without having shivers run down my spine. If there's a single event recorded in Scripture—other than Jesus' own death and resurrection—that points to who He is and what He came to do, it has to be the death and resurrection of Lazarus. And yet many questions and challenges lie embedded in the story. Our Lord evidently knew all along how events would unfold and the part He would play in them. In fact, He waited on purpose for Lazarus to die before He and His disciples left for Bethany. He even told the Twelve, "I am glad for your sakes that I was not there, so that you may believe" (John 11:15). But He did not explain His plan to the disciples. Nor did He tell Martha what He would do. He did not apologize. Instead, His words almost teased her with the truth: "Your brother shall rise again" (v. 23).

Our Lord's actions and His remarks all point toward a single message: "Trust Me, even when the circumstances shout that I'm untrustworthy." The events of John 11 unfold like a well-planned object lesson or a classic laboratory exercise. Jesus wanted the disciples to remember forever a handful of bedrock truths. Instead of just explaining these principles, He led the Twelve (and Mary and Martha) through an exercise to illustrate them.

As we pray for God's help with problems such as illnesses, financial needs, and family challenges, we too can stand firm on these foundational truths. They will protect us from discouragement and will spur us on toward persistence in prayer. Let's look at each of them in detail.

Truth 1—Everything God does for His children is done in love.

Inspired by the Holy Spirit, the apostle John records the story of Lazarus in a curious way. Take, for instance, the footnote John adds after he explains the arrival of the messenger and the announcement that Lazarus is ill. John goes on to say:

> *Jesus loved Martha, and her sister, and Lazarus. When therefore He heard that he was sick, He stayed then two days longer in the place where He was. (vv. 5–6)*

What a juxtaposition! Jesus loved Martha, Mary, and Lazarus—so He waited until, humanly speaking, it was too late to help them. You see, Jesus had something even greater in mind for this little family than they could then imagine. And He was up to something more than they could then see. He didn't want Lazarus to be merely another statistic in the long line of healing miracles He performed while He walked here on earth. He wanted to demonstrate for Lazarus—and for thousands and millions of believers down through history—the full extent of His love and power. He wanted to show Mary and Martha that He is *always* able and willing to help us—even when human help is impossible, unthinkable.

Do you suppose Mary and Martha would have wanted this incident to turn out some other way? Knowing what they knew at the end of the story, would they have preferred that Jesus had come immediately? Would they have chosen to have Him perform one of the long-distance healings He was famous for? I don't think so. As wrenching as Lazarus' death surely was, neither Martha nor Mary nor Lazarus himself would have missed the ending for all the world.

Jesus loved Martha and her sister and Lazarus, so He waited two days before He set out for Bethany.

Truth 2—When God's perfect time arrives, nothing can keep Him from acting.

When Jesus finally did announce to the Twelve that it was time to go to help Lazarus, the disciples tried to deter Him. Bethany, you see, lay in the province of Judea, only two miles from Jerusalem. They reminded the Lord: *"Rabbi, the Jews were just now seeking to stone You, and are You going there again?"* (v. 8)

Jesus' enemies in Jerusalem had begun to plot His destruction. But Jesus went there anyway. His friends needed Him. And the time to do the Father's will had come. None of the events had taken God by surprise. Not the attitudes of Jesus' enemies. Not the illness and death of Lazarus. Not the fears or anger or doubts or hurt of Martha and Mary. Nothing in our lives takes God by surprise either. And when the time comes for Him to help His friends today—that's us according to John 15:15—nothing will stop Him. His will, including His timing, is "good and acceptable and perfect" (Romans 12:2).

Truth 3—Our pain touches and moves the heart of God.

As Jesus stood outside the tomb of Lazarus, He wept (John 11:35). He wept openly. He wept over the sorrow and misery that sin and death had brought into our world. And He wept specifically for Martha and Mary in their pain. Do you suppose your Savior, the one who has called you His own brother, His own sister, His own friend, has any less compassion for you than He had for them? The apostle James writes:

> The Lord is full of compassion and is merciful. (James 5:11)

As we bring our own needs and the needs of others before our Lord, we can be sure He will meet us at heaven's gates, so to speak. He anxiously awaits our requests. The Bible says:

> Therefore the LORD longs to be gracious to you,
> And therefore He waits on high
>   to have compassion on you.
> For the LORD is a God of justice;
> How blessed are all those who long for Him.
> (Isaiah 30:18)

Truth 4—God is not only always willing to help, He is always able to help.

Jesus demonstrated His divine power when He stood outside Lazarus' tomb that day in Bethany. Most of us have had the experience of wanting to help someone, but finding their situation far beyond our ability to change it. Had we visited in Bethany, you and I could have handed Martha and Mary fresh handkerchiefs. We could have held them while they cried on our shoulder. We could have listened while they spoke of their grief. But that's about our limit. That's about all we could have done for them. Jesus not only raised Lazarus that day, He pointed toward an even greater miracle—one that benefits us already and that will continue to benefit you and me throughout all eternity:

> Jesus said … "I am the resurrection and the life; he who believes in Me shall live even if he dies, and everyone who lives and believes in Me shall never die." (John 11:25–26)

A god who was willing to help us in our need, but unable to do so would be pitiful, unworthy of worship. A god who was able to help, but unwilling to do so would be a tyrant, too cruel to worship. Our God is both willing and able. He is even "able to do exceeding abundantly beyond all that we ask or think" (Ephesians 3:20).

Because all four principles are true, we can do what the writer to the Hebrews invites us to do:

> Let us therefore draw near with confidence to the throne of grace, that we may receive mercy and may find grace to help in time of need. (Hebrews 4:16)

What Can We Expect?

When we pray as the children of God through Jesus Christ, we can expect that God will hear and answer us.

Based on the biblical truths outlined above and on the examples of God's actions in response to His people's prayers recorded for us in the Holy Scriptures, it's fair to say that God answers prayer in one of two ways.

First, He often says yes. He often does just what we ask. Sometimes He does this even before we think to ask Him. In fact, He says this about His people's prayers: "Before they call, I will answer; and while they are still speaking, I will hear" (Isaiah 65:24). Remember King Hezekiah? He hadn't even finished asking for healing when the Lord spoke from heaven to the prophet Isaiah, promising to add 15 years to the king's life.

The secular world around us would have us believe we live in a closed universe, one in which God either does not or cannot intervene. Such people pooh-pooh the possibility of miracles. Where we see our prayers being answered, they see only chance or coincidence at work. Sad to say, some even in the church have come to discount the possibility of God "meddling in the affairs of earth." Such people see prayer as a way God changes us and our attitudes, rather than as a way we can participate in His purposes for people or as a way we can influence events and circumstances. How sad. How much peace and joy such people miss on their journey through life.

A few years ago when my nephews and nieces were younger, I stopped at the home of one of my sisters after a long drive. It was close to midnight and I was tired. My sister met me at the door and apologized for not inviting me in. Her three-year-old daughter had a virulent form of the flu. Kristin was running a 105 degree fever and had been miserable all day. The pediatrician, apparently busy with other children suffering from a similar malady, had not returned any of their phone calls. Gail urged me to find a motel so that I wouldn't be exposed to a virus that could force me to spend the upcoming Christmas holiday sick in bed.

I found myself instantly angry. How dare Satan conspire to ruin the family time I had been looking forward to? How dare he hurt my niece and cause her family such concern? Instead of leaving, I asked Gail if I could pray with Kristin. The little girl looked as pale and weak and miserable as you might imagine a three-year-old would look after fighting such a fever all day long. I felt even angrier at the devil as I reached down to hold Kristin's hand. I asked her if she knew of any people Jesus had healed. She said yes and told a condensed but accurate version of Jesus healing Jairus' daughter. Then we prayed together, asking Jesus to do for Kristin what He had done for that other little girl so long ago. After the prayer, Gail and I went to the kitchen for a cup of tea. Not 10 minutes later, Kristin walked out. She said, "Mommy, I'm hungry." She ate a bowl of chicken noodle soup and drank two glasses of grape juice. Her fever was gone. She slept 12 hours, and that was the end of that. Around 1:00 A.M., the pediatrician called, bleary-eyed, from the hospital. Gail told him we didn't need him anymore, but thank you. Our true Physician made a housecall that night. I have no doubt.

I have a friend who lived through the Great Depression. She tells about sitting down at the table at mealtime with no food in the house. After the family had prayed a prayer of thanks to God for their meal, they sat and looked at one another. Then they heard a knock at the door. When they opened it, they found no one—only a bag full of oranges. They ate them—for lunch and, later on that evening, for supper.

Would Kristin have recovered without our prayer? Would the oranges have arrived had my friend's family not prayed? And why didn't God supply bread, ham, and cheese besides the oranges? I don't know. If we wait to pray until we have all our questions answered, we will never get around to praying. Kristin did get well. My friend's family did not go to bed hungry. God does answer many of our prayers with an immediate and enthusiastic YES! He does this because He loves us, and He loves to help us. Jesus loves to answer prayer. And when He does, we praise and honor Him for it. We give Him the credit, the glory, because He's the one who rightly deserves it. It's not that we're such great prayer warriors. It's not that we have such great faith. It's not that we've managed to mouth just the right formula or to repeat it often enough. It's that He's promised to "supply all your needs according to His riches in glory in Christ Jesus" (Philippians 4:19), and He honors us by letting us participate in His process of doing that as we pray.

God often says yes. And He answers prayer in one other way too. Often He says, "I've heard what you've asked. But I have something even better in mind." That's the answer Jesus used in the case of Martha, Mary, and Lazarus, wasn't it? At the time, it didn't look like God's way was a better way. In fact, God's way looked like a disaster. It looked as though no one in the whole enterprise would ever recover. Martha and Mary would never get their brother back. Jesus would never get His reputation back. And Jesus' followers would never regain their confidence in Him. For four days, the situation looked about as grim as any situation can look. But God knew all along what He would do.

Countless saints have seen our Lord use even the craftiest schemes of Satan for the good of His saints. Think of their testimonies! Both the Old and New Testaments are full of their life stories, and in nearly every one of those stories we see that someone—or many someones—prayed. Satan came and kept coming to "steal, kill, and destroy" in the lives of God's people (John 10:10). But he never succeeded. And he never will.

God's people sometimes face grim facts. The doctor says, "Terminal." The accountant says, "Bankrupt." The supervisor says, "Fired." The judge says, "Divorced." But even then, and especially then, we can rely on the fact that God has committed Himself to help us, to stand on our side, to deliver us. Remember that promise from Romans 8?

He who did not spare His own Son, but delivered Him up for us all, how will He not also with Him freely give us all things? (v. 32)

God promises to hear and to answer our prayers—

all our prayers. Sometimes He calms the storm; sometimes He calms His child. But always He is "our refuge and strength, A very present help in trouble" (Psalm 46:1). He's not just present, He's present to help—in every kind of trouble. When the sky darkens and angry clouds begin to gather in our lives or in the lives of those we love, we can—in full confidence—trust Him to bring us through, keep us safe, and bring us home to Himself in the end.

LOOKING AHEAD

God always hears when we pray. But it can sometimes seem that He's not listening. And sometimes we hesitate to talk to Him because of what's going on inside us. When we're angry (especially if we're angry at Him), anxious (especially when we know we should be trusting Him), or disappointed (especially when we're not so thrilled with what He seems to be doing), it's hard to make ourselves pray. It's hard to believe His Word that we're "armed and dangerous" as far as Satan is concerned.

Still, those can be times we most need to pray, and they can be times when genuine, honest prayer can help us the most. What does an angry or discouraged Christian say to God? Read on; chapter 8 details the answer to that question.

LOOKING INWARD AND UPWARD

The questions below may stimulate a lot of thought, a lot of self-examination. You will probably find that process most helpful if you talk it out with another believer, someone whom you trust. Be as honest as you can with yourself and your partner as you think out loud together.

- The prayer group sat down one Monday evening as they had done every week for the past five years. The leader began going over the list of needs for which members of the congregation had requested prayer. After several minutes, one member of the group interrupted. "We've prayed for some of these situations for years!" she said. "Some of the family problems go on and on. Some of the people are still sick—or even sicker. Some of these people still need a new job. Or, they need another new job. I don't get it. Just what *is* supposed to happen when we pray for all these needs!?" If you sat in this group, how would you answer?

- Tell about a time God answered one of your prayers, "YES!"

- Tell about a time God answered one of your prayers, "I want to give you something even better." Did it seem better to you right away? If so, what did you learn from that? If not, what did you learn?

- As you pray right now, for what answers to prayer would you especially like to thank your Lord?

PRACTICAL PRAYER TIP

What do you do when someone you care about has wandered from the faith or is caught in some sin? In

Matthew 18, Jesus prescribes some actions we can take. Then He connects this promise with those actions:

> *If two of you agree on earth about anything that they may ask, it shall be done for them by My Father who is in heaven.* (v. 19)

If you've been praying about a loved one in spiritual danger, perhaps now would be a good time to invite someone to pray with you. And perhaps the two of you could talk about what actions the Lord Jesus might want you—empowered by His grace—to take.

8

PRAYING THROUGH ANGER AND DISCOURAGEMENT

No one knows what provoked the outburst. Perhaps a sudden disaster had flooded his life, a disaster that threatened to drown him in an ocean of grief. Or, perhaps a dozen minor irritations were nibbling him to death, darting around his head like sand fleas, never leaving him alone, not even in his sleep.

The details of the problem don't matter, not really. What counts is that he ran to God, not away from Him.

And God listened. In fact, He saw fit to record the prayer so you and I could eavesdrop, and so we could use those same words ourselves when we need to. Not when we feel sweet and close to God and pious. But when, like David, we're steamed and frustrated and feel like throwing things. This is the prayer David prayed:

How long, O LORD? Wilt Thou forget me forever?
How long wilt Thou hide Thy face from me?
How long shall I take counsel in my soul,
Having sorrow in my heart all the day?
How long will my enemy be exalted over me?
Consider and answer me, O LORD, my God;
Enlighten my eyes, lest I sleep the sleep of death,
Lest my enemy say, "I have overcome him,"
Lest my adversaries rejoice when I am shaken.
(Psalm 13:1–4)

Brain research stands out as one of the most fascinating fields of study today. As biologists and physiologists continue to map the human brain and to learn more about how it works, it becomes more and more evident that our emotions are key to nearly everything we do. Emotion drives attention. And attention, in turn, drives memory, learning, and problem-solving. We may like to think of ourselves as logical beings whose rationality is sometimes overridden by a surge of emotion during a time of crisis. But most scientists now believe that just the opposite is true, that our emotional system is our default system, the one on which we most rely as we move through our days and our lives.

Of course, none of this research took our Creator

by surprise. He knows the power of emotions in our decisions and in our relationships—especially in our relationship with Him. Perhaps that's why so much of the Bible is written in the language of emotion—the language of poetry. The Psalms. Isaiah. Job. Micah. Malachi. Jeremiah. Hosea. The list goes on and on. Substantial portions of many Bible books package the truths God intends to convey in powerful images, images designed to provoke emotions—revulsion at sin, peace in God's pardon, anger at injustice, awe at the majesty of God, and so on.

Now certainly the truths of God remain true, regardless of our feelings at any given moment. (And how glad we can be about that!) But as we enter the throne room of our Lord, we need not check our hearts at the door. Even if we could do that, even if we could consistently come into His presence to pray with dispassion, He would not want us to pray that way. How do we know? For one thing, we can take a long look at the prayers He's chosen to record for us in the Bible.

David, the "man after God's own heart" (see Acts 13:22), wrote dozens of prayer-songs that express all the anxiety, all the joy, all the fear, all the awe, all the anger, all the hope, all the discouragement, and all the contentment a human heart can feel. Or, remember King Hezekiah and the prayer he prayed through his tears (Isaiah 38)? Or Hannah—Samuel's mother—who prayed with such feeling that the priest, Eli, accused her of being drunk (1 Samuel 1:9–18). Or Jesus Himself who prayed through such sorrow and with such intensity that "His sweat became like drops of blood, falling down upon the ground" (Luke 22:44). No, we need not check our hearts at the door when we come to our Lord in prayer.

Still, some emotions, left unresolved, can get in the way of our relationship with God. They can block or stifle our prayers to Him. Let's look at two of the emotions most likely to do that and think about how to pray when we're in the throes of anger or discouragement.

Dear God, I'm Angry!

The thought of praying while angry offends some Christians. It frightens others. Even so, anger is a fact of life. God knows this. The Lord warned Cain about the dangers of anger just before Cain killed his brother Abel. God watched as a young Moses fell into a fit of rage, murdered an Egyptian, and buried his victim in a shallow grave. God saw Israel's first king, Saul, spin out of control in anger as he hurled spears at David and later at his own son, Jonathan. Anger easily leads to rage and from rage to hatred and from hatred to homicide.

On the other hand, not all anger is in and of itself sinful. God Himself gets angry. The Scriptures describe His holy anger at disobedience and injustice. Anger has often motivated God's people to stand up for the innocent and to right wrongs. The things that anger God should anger us too—violence, useless pain, blasphemy, indifference to God, lovelessness—all these and more are at their core works of Satan, God's enemy and ours. Satan and his works can rightly evoke our anger, just as they evoke God's.

That fact lies behind those psalms that puzzle and sometimes embarrass Christians. We call these psalms "imprecatory psalms" because they call down imprecations—curses—on evildoers. These prayers shock those who define Christianity as simply a lifestyle of "being nice" to people and not rocking any boats. But Christians have never worshiped a "nice" God. We worship a God of grace who acts in perfect justice. He sent His own dear Son to suffer the punishment all human beings have earned for themselves by their sins. How glad we are to know that! But those who reject His gift of forgiveness and who refuse to bow to His lordship will one day receive the judgment they deserve. That grieves God, and it grieves us, but it will happen nonetheless.

We shudder when we think of it. But we also shake our heads in disgust as we see the misery Satan and his human allies inflict on the children of God. When we hear about little children being murdered, when we read about Christians who are tortured for the faith, when we watch the bodies of our loved ones being racked by cancer, when we see drugs pull teenagers into the sewer and alcohol amputate moms or dads from their families, when these things and things like them happen, we can and do find ourselves rightly outraged.

A part of the baptismal service used by the church from ancient times onward asked the person being baptized to "renounce the devil and all his works and all his ways." When we see Satan's works and recognize his ways playing themselves out in the lives of those we love, we renew our renunciation of Satan. We not only renounce him, we denounce him as the thief and murderer he truly is (John 10:10).

But God invites us to do more. We can bring the problem, the need to Him. Even if we're angry, even if our anger is all tangled up with the problem, even if we can't find the words to explain ourselves rationally, we can come to our Father with it. Here's His invitation:

Trust in Him at all times, O people;
Pour out your heart before Him;
God is a refuge for us. (Psalm 62:8)

Our Lord wants us to see Him as an ally. He stands squarely on our side and against the works and ways of Satan. He shares our anger at those works and ways. In fact, Satan's work angers Him even more than it angers us. He has done something about it—in Jesus our Savior. And He will keep acting on behalf of His children as we battle the forces of darkness. One day, Satan will find himself flung into the lake of fire God has prepared for him and his angels. On that day, true justice, pure justice will prevail. That fact can comfort us in our anger at earth's misery.

So holy anger can play a rightful part in our prayer lives. But there's another kind of anger too.

Angry at God?

The question is not so much *do* God's children sometimes get angry at Him, the question is what do we do when we are. If you believe God loves you; if you believe He's the "living God," the God who acts on behalf of His children; if you believe He's all-powerful and all-wise; then chances are good that at sometime in life you will fail to see His wisdom in allowing some pain, some problem, some disappointment to continue. When that happens, you will find yourself becoming angry, angry at the injury and angry at God for not intervening right away.

Remember Job? He's famous in some circles for his purported patience. And yet, from chapter 3 onward, Job continually says some very impatient things. If today's supermarket tabloids had been in publication back in Job's day, their headlines would have screamed something like this:

Former Preacher Demands New Trial in Heaven's Court
'Kill Me Now, God' Insists Ancient Evangelist

Despite Job's angry words, despite all the times he shook his fist at heaven, the Lord acted in mercy toward Job. In fact, the book of Job reveals a whole lot more about God's patience than about Job's. But why did the Holy Spirit see fit to record the events at all? What purpose does it serve for God's people to read more than 40 chapters, most of those detailing Job's complaints that God has treated him unfairly?

For one thing, it can give us the confidence we need to go to God when we ourselves feel He is being harsh or unjust with us. True, Job foolishly flung unfounded accusations at our Lord. He demanded God hear his case; he moved from wishing he'd never been born to begging God for death; he griped about not having a higher court to which he could appeal heaven's verdicts. The Lord could have swatted him like a fly—and justly too. But He didn't. He listened. Any human listener would have gotten defensive, but God didn't. The Lord's only concern was helping the one whom He called from beginning to end "My servant Job" (1:8, 42:7). Even at its worst, Job's anger couldn't stop God's love for him.

Just about any believer, tormented long enough and hard enough, will find himself or herself getting as angry as Job got. God knows when we're angry at Him. He knows it even before we do, and He knows it whether we tell Him so or not. Satan usually knows it too. He schemes to keep our anger simmering deep down inside ourselves. Satan wants us to pull away from our Lord, to let our anger become a wall that will shut God out. That surely was Satan's plan for Job, and it nearly succeeded. God, on the other hand, wants us to come to Him just as we are, anger and all. He wants to use our anger as an impetus to find out more about His Word and His ways. That way, when our anger has passed, our relationship with Him will be—by His grace—even deeper and fuller. Remember His invitation:

> Trust in Him at all times, O people;
> Pour out your heart before Him;
> God is a refuge for us. (Psalm 62:8)

We can trust Him at *all* times, yes, even times of anger and frustration. We can pour out our hearts before His throne. Even when our hearts are full of bitterness and resentment, we can pour those things out before Him. And when we do, we will find Him to be a merciful and forgiving Savior. We will find in Him a Friend to wipe away our tears, to ease our heartache, to assure us of His eternal love, and to join us on the battlefield against the evil that taunts us. That's the message of Job as the Holy Spirit Himself interprets it through the apostle James:

> You have heard of the endurance of Job and have seen the outcome of the Lord's dealings, that the Lord is full of compassion and is merciful. (James 5:11)

Dear God, I'm Discouraged

David asked the "how long" question four different times in the psalm you read at the beginning of this chapter. It's not only a question of frustration or anger, it's also a question we ask when we find ourselves discouraged. Discouragement can kill the joy God wants us to have in Jesus. It's a prayer-killer too. Have you ever been too discouraged to pray?

Discouragement often comes when we find ourselves praying for the same thing for a long time, seemingly without results. For instance, maybe you've been asking God to bring your wife to faith in Him. Or, maybe you've been asking your Lord to heal your diabetes or chronic pain. Maybe you have been wrestling in prayer for a personal victory over some long-term addiction to gambling or pornography or compulsive spending. Maybe you've been interceding for a neighbor who has suffered from depression for decades. Or, maybe you have prayed that God would find a way to get an innocent friend released from prison.

Whenever we pray for a situation that doesn't resolve itself in a few days or a few weeks or a few months, or a few years, we're likely candidates for discouragement. This can show up in any one of several ways. We can find ourselves tempted to give up, to give in to fatalism, as we tell ourselves, "I guess this was just meant to be." We can begin to avoid contact with our Lord. Perhaps we still take ourselves to church, but we stop paying attention. Perhaps we still read our Bible, but approach it as if it were just another human book. Perhaps we still pray, but we stop expecting it to do any good.

Or, we can find ourselves steeped in worry. Having turned the situation over to our Lord in prayer "once and for all," we can find ourselves taking it back again, trying to figure it out on our own, trying to manipulate people or circumstances so that they line up with our view of the way things ought to be.

Or, we can find ourselves devoid of feeling. It can seem that our prayers bounce off the ceiling and back to earth rather than ascending to the very throne of God. We can conclude that our Lord hasn't heard or even that He doesn't care. But the fact is, He does care. He's told us so. In any case, we cannot know for sure at any given time how close God's answer may be.

A friend and I hiked a path through one of Missouri's state parks one day. We had wanted an hour's peace, strolling through the trees and photographing spring flowers. What we got was a hike that went on for more than three hours and took us trotting up and down steep ravines. The path was supposed to loop around to bring us back to the place we had parked the car. We kept debating whether to turn around and go back the way we had come. But we kept telling each other, "We've got to be there any minute. We've almost made it. Let's keep on going." Finally, we decided we had to give up and turn back. Just then we met some hikers coming down the path toward us. They told us what we needed to hear. The parking lot was 50 yards straight ahead, hidden from our view by a tangle of trees and tall bushes.

Whenever you're discouraged in your prayers, remember this: You don't know how far you've come. For all you know, your Father is even now sending one of His holy angels to do for you just exactly what you've been asking all these weeks and months and years. David didn't end Psalm 13 with the "how long" question. He ended it with a refrain of faith. Let the Holy Spirit use David's words to refresh and encourage you:

> But I have trusted in Thy lovingkindness;
> My heart shall rejoice in Thy salvation.
> I will sing to the LORD,
> Because He has dealt bountifully with me. (vv. 5–6)

Looking Ahead

In our "just do it" culture, prayer can seem less vital than action. Perhaps you're a pastor. Perhaps you teach a Sunday school class or lead an adult Bible study group. Maybe you organize the volunteers who visit shut-ins in the congregation. Or, possibly you serve the Lord Jesus by making evangelism calls. Whatever you do in the church, you probably find that you're tempted to focus on planning more than praying, on intervening and interacting more than on interceding. But that can be a drastic mistake. Chapter 9 will help you discern the help the Lord intends prayer to be for you as you serve Him.

Looking Inward and Upward

Think about these questions prayerfully. Talk with your prayer partner or with others in your prayer group about them if you can. See what you can learn from each other.

- Does it surprise you to know that you "needn't check your heart at the door" when you come into God's presence to pray? Explain.
- When are you most likely to find yourself angry at God or discouraged in your prayers? What helps when that happens?
- Reread Psalm 13 in its entirety. Does the psalm comfort you? surprise you? give you any new insights? Explain.
- Based on what you've read in this chapter

about anger and discouragement, what would you most like to say to God as you pray right now?

PRACTICAL PRAYER TIP

Take 30 minutes or so sometime soon and use it to skim through the book of Psalms. Look for words that you would find helpful in times of anger or discouragement. Mark them somehow or make a note of those you've found in your prayer journal. Then pray them when you need to.

9

PRAYER IS NOT A PRELUDE

The crowd was fast becoming a mob. Violence would not lag far behind. The prosperity, the peace, the glory they thought they had been promised had turned to dust. Their dreams had become ashes in their mouths. That's how they saw it. And they said so in no uncertain terms.

Their leaders didn't try to argue. They didn't preach a sermon. They didn't form a grievance committee. Instead, they fell on their faces, prostrate before the Lord—in honor of His name, in humility, and in hope.

They prayed instead of trying to persuade. They interceded instead of trying to intervene. They remind-

ed God of His promises instead of reviling the people for their rebellion. And the God of grace heard. He pardoned. He commuted the death sentence the whole community deserved.

The next 40 years would be no picnic for Moses and Aaron. Or for the people, for that matter. They would suffer the fate they had accused God of planning for their children; their dead bodies would fall in the wilderness. And all because they had failed to trust God's Word, His promises. But the Lord would use the wilderness wanderings they were about to begin to teach Israel His ways. He would give them another chance to trust. And another. And yet another. Aaron—and Moses too—would eventually die in the desert like those they led. But God would use their lives and their witness to glorify Himself as He formed and shaped their hearts, their minds, their characters, and then as He took them each to Himself in Canaan above.

A careful reading of Exodus, Numbers, and Deuteronomy shows that prayer was not a prelude to the ministry God did through Moses and Aaron as they led the children of Israel out of Egypt and into the land the Lord had promised to give Abraham, Isaac, and Jacob. In a real sense, prayer itself *was* their ministry. Time and again these two—prophet and priest—fell on their faces in the sand before God, unashamed to show their helplessness to the people they led. Whenever the disaster of disobedience arose, Moses and Aaron resorted to intercession.

The case recorded in Numbers 14:1–35 typifies

this response. Perhaps you recall some of the details about that day. The spies had just returned from surveying Canaan. Ten of the 12 brought a report reminiscent of those medieval maps that warned sailors away from the edges of the earth by reporting, "There be dragons ..." The 10 said nothing about dragons, but they worried aloud about giants. The people, ever suspicious of the Lord, ignored a minority report by Joshua and Caleb that encouraged them to believe their God and take their Promised Land. Instead, they wailed about the danger and whined in doubt and discouragement.

While Joshua and Caleb tried to calm the mob's fears, Moses and Aaron prayed. Moses quoted God's promises back to Him:

> But now, I pray, let the power of the Lord be great, just as Thou hast declared, "The LORD is slow to anger and abundant in lovingkindness, forgiving iniquity and transgression; but He will by no means clear the guilty, visiting the iniquity of the fathers on the children to the third and the fourth generations." Pardon, I pray, the iniquity of this people according to the greatness of Thy lovingkindness, just as Thou also hast forgiven this people, from Egypt even until now. (vv. 17–19)

God did, as we have seen, pardon. But the die was cast. The wilderness would be home to Israel as over the next 40 years the scenario begun at Kadesh Barnia repeated itself time and again. Never once did Moses try to defend himself or his actions. Instead, he prayed.

The Posture of Personal Weakness

If Moses needed to pray as he served God's people, how much do we ourselves need it as we serve others in Christ's name? "Who am I," he had asked of Yahweh at the burning bush, "that I should go to Pharaoh and lead the children of Israel out of Egypt?" From day 1 Moses knew—to the point of pain—his own insufficiency, his own weakness. That knowledge drove him to his knees. That knowledge threw him on his face before his God and before those whom he led. And that knowledge forged a chain linking Moses with St. Paul and with all God's servants down through history who have been led by God to recognize their inability to minister in their own strength. This recognition strips us too of all *self*-confidence and places us squarely on the mercy of God even as we serve Him. It lifts the pressure for results off our shoulders and places responsibility for outcomes where it belongs—in the hands of our gracious God:

> And such confidence we have through Christ toward God. Not that we are adequate in ourselves to consider anything as coming from ourselves, but our adequacy is from God, who also made us adequate as servants of a new covenant. (2 Corinthians 3:4–6)

We serve a God infinite in glory, in strength, in wisdom, in grace, in understanding, in love. But we ourselves are not infinite, not even close. When we pretend we are, when we ignore our finitude, we drive ourselves quickly to the breaking point. When we fail to recognize and admit our limits, we sin. A wise person once cautioned me, "The world has one Savior; you're not Him."

True freedom and real joy in service come when we face our helplessness, when we admit the futility of trying to do God's work our way or through our own abilities. This confession opens the way by which we can access the infinite resources of heaven. How many "crisis conferences" have you attended in churches in which the group prayed for 30 seconds and anguished over solutions for three hours? We do not have the answers for those we lead, regardless of whether those we serve are third-graders in a Sunday school class, teens in a service group, or the members of a congregation of 3,000 souls. If we ourselves act as guide, neither we nor those we lead will ever make it out of the wilderness. But the good news is that though we are not adequate in and of ourselves …

> *Our adequacy is from God, who also made us adequate as servants of a new covenant.* (2 Corinthians 3:5–6)

The blessing of recognizing this truth comes to us as God's gift. As God works in us through His Word and by the power of His Spirit, we begin to realize more and more our need for God's direction. We begin to see our service in a new light. Our goal becomes simply leading others into God's presence so that *He* can minister to them. That becomes more and more the focus of our prayers as the Holy Spirit peels our fingers one by one off the cliff of self-sufficiency so that we can fall back into His grace, safe and at peace with ourselves and with the role God has given to us.

Christ Must Increase

Stand in the sandals of John the Baptizer for a moment. Imagine that your people have just come through a 500-year period during which no prophet has arisen. God has been present, but He has been silent. Now He has touched you and filled you to overflowing with the Holy Spirit. Fire burns in your soul just as it burned in the soul of the great prophet Elijah! The kingdom of God is about to dawn. The King will soon reveal Himself. Your God-given task is to prepare your people for the coming of that kingdom, that King.

Consider the temptation to tout yourself and your calling under such circumstances. "God's Man of Great Faith and Power"—you fit the description! And yet John the Baptizer rejected that mantle. He refused to let anyone drape it across his shoulders. He pointed his disciples to Christ, saying, "He must increase, but I must decrease" (John 3:30). Many, perhaps most or even all of John's followers, drifted away after that. They sat down at the feet of a different Teacher. Did that disappoint John? Would it disappoint you?

Our sinful nature would, no doubt, grimace at the possibility. Still, we know a sincere pleasure, a holy pleasure, when we see those we lead begin to look, not to us, but to Jesus. That's our goal for them. What's more, it's *God's* goal for them too. Our prayers play an important part in their growth toward that goal. At least two outstanding things happen as we pray.

For one thing, as we pray aloud with and for those who sit under our teaching, under our counsel, under our spiritual leadership, we show them in a direct way God's goal for their lives. Our prayers help them recognize the true and only Source of help, of hope. The prayers we pray when we are with them remind those we serve that even when we're not around, they can still access all the help of heaven.

Secondly, our prayers for those to whom we minister remind us of how dependent we are on our Savior-God as we serve His people. God promises:

> Behold I lay in Zion a choice stone, a precious corner stone,
> And he who believes in Him shall not be disappointed.
> (1 Peter 2:6)

Those who put their trust in Christ will not be disappointed. We can rely on that promise both for ourselves and for those whom we lead. Whatever challenges of faith or life people face, the strength and wisdom to meet those challenges must and will come from God's throne of grace. Even when people can't or won't pray for themselves, we can access heaven on their behalf. Prayer isn't an adjunct, a frill, an auxiliary part of our service. In a real way, it *is* our service, our primary responsibility and privilege as we serve. And even if it weren't, our own need and our Father's promise would certainly draw us, drive us even, to His throne.

Remind Me!

Such intercession pleases Him—immensely. The most powerful of God's servants paralleled their prophetic call with a call to prayer. We've seen that in the case of Moses. But scan the book of Jeremiah. Study the life of Elijah. Consider the ministry of Daniel. Think about Abraham. Picture Paul agonizing in prayer for the Colossians and those in all the churches to whom he ministered. Then meditate on the fact that our Lord Jesus Himself ascended to heaven for the express purpose of interceding for us! That ministry occupies His heart and mind continually—right up to and including this very moment!

One of the saddest passages in all the Old Testament describes one of God's biggest disappointments. Our Lord says:

> I searched for a man among them who should build up the wall and stand in the gap before Me for the land, that I should not destroy it; but I found no one. (Ezekiel 22:30)

One person on his knees, one person on her face could have made a difference at this juncture in Israel's history. God looked for such a person; no one was to be found. But the story does not end in bad news. Listen!

> Now the LORD saw, … that there was no man,
> And was astonished that
>   there was no one to intercede;
> Then His own arm brought salvation to Him;
> And His righteousness upheld Him.
> And He put on righteousness like a breastplate,
> And a helmet of salvation on His head;
> And He put on garments of vengeance for clothing,
> And wrapped Himself with zeal as a mantle. …

He will come like a rushing stream,
Which the wind of the LORD drives.
And a Redeemer will come to Zion, ...

"And as for Me, this is My covenant with them," says
the LORD: "My Spirit which is upon you, and My words
which I have put in your mouth, shall not depart from
your mouth, nor from the mouth of your offspring, nor
from the mouth of your offspring's offspring," says the
LORD, "from now and forever." (Isaiah 59:15–21)

Jesus came as a mighty Warrior to meet our desperate needs both for a Redeemer and for an Intercessor. He strapped on His mighty armor and went to battle with Satan. He won. It's no accident that Paul describes that very same armor in Ephesians 6, and as he does so, he tells us that in Christ we now have the right, the privilege, the obligation really, to wear it. Because we are united with Christ, the armor of Christ and the victory of Christ now belong to us. And it's no accident that wearing and using that armor is inextricably tied up in intercessory prayer. Recall that connection, first noted in chapter 1 of this book, as you read:

Take up the full armor of God, that you may be able to
resist in the evil day, and having done everything, to
stand firm. Stand firm therefore, having girded your
loins with truth, and having put on the breastplate of
righteousness, and having shod your feet with the
preparation of the gospel of peace; in addition to all,
taking up the shield of faith with which you will be able
to extinguish all the flaming missiles of the evil one. And
take the helmet of salvation, and the sword of the Spir-

*it, which is the word of God. **With all prayer and petition pray at all times in the Spirit,** and with this in view, be on the alert with all perseverance and petition for all the saints, and pray on my behalf, that utterance may be given to me in the opening of my mouth, to make known with boldness the mystery of the gospel.* (Ephesians 6:13–19, emphasis added)

Confident in Christ, we intercede for our own service and for the service others give in Christ's name. As we do that, we obey God, we please God, we become more like Christ, we receive power for our service, and we participate in the coming of the kingdom of Christ. God is looking for intercessors. God is looking for those who will cry out to Him for "Jerusalem," for "Zion"—for His people, His church, His kingdom. How will you respond to that invitation of grace?

On your walls, O Jerusalem,
I have appointed watchmen;
All day and all night they will never keep silent.
You who remind the LORD, take no rest for yourselves;
And give Him no rest until He establishes
And makes Jerusalem a praise in the earth.
(Isaiah 62:6–7)

LOOKING AHEAD

Is prayer a dialog or a monolog? When you pray could you just as well put your thoughts down in a fax or zing it heavenward via e-mail? Or, is prayer more like a conversation with your dad or wife or best friend? The next chapter will work through this issue.

Looking Inward and Upward

Think about these questions prayerfully. Talk with your prayer partner or with others in your prayer group about them if you can. See what you discover.

- Think of a time you fell back on prayer as your only recourse as you served God's people, a time when all you could do was pray. What did you learn from that experience?
- Why do you suppose even mature Christian leaders sometimes fall into the temptation of putting prayer on a back burner so that they have time to get to "the real ministry"?
- Would your schedule change if you honestly believed the principles laid out in this chapter regarding prayer and Christian service? Explain.
- Based on your answers to the questions above, what would you like to say to the Lord—your mighty, saving, victorious, protecting, forgiving Warrior-God?

Practical Prayer Tip

Posture matters when we pray. God created us as physical creatures, and we can use our bodies as well as our souls to honor Him. Kneeling signals something different than standing when we pray. Lying on one's face affects a person differently than sitting with hands raised. As you pray, experiment with different postures. Of course, God hears us regardless of whether we stand, sit, or kneel. But different postures can be an aid to *us* as we approach Him.

10

HEARING GOD SPEAK WHEN WE PRAY

My voice rises to God, and I will cry aloud;
My voice rises to God, and He will hear me.
In the day of my trouble I sought the Lord;
In the night my hand was stretched out
    without weariness;
My soul refused to be comforted.
When I remember God, then I am disturbed;
When I sigh, then my spirit grows faint. ...

Will the LORD reject forever?
And will He never be favorable again?

Has His lovingkindness ceased forever?
Has His promise come to an end forever?
Has God forgotten to be gracious?
Or has He in anger withdrawn
      His compassion? ...
I shall remember the deeds of the LORD;
Surely I will remember Thy wonders of old.
I will meditate on all Thy work,
And muse on Thy deeds.
Thy way, O God, is holy;
What god is great like our God?
Thou art the God who workest wonders;
Thou hast made known Thy strength among the
      peoples.
Thou hast by Thy power redeemed Thy people,
The sons of Jacob and Joseph.
(Excerpted from Psalm 77:1–15)

Do you ever read between the lines when you get an e-mail message or receive a letter from someone close to you? When we do that, we're not concentrating on the white spaces on the page; we're looking for nuances in words and for feelings behind sentences to add information to the facts expressed on the surface.

We do it when we read Scripture too. Of course, we must take care not to read in things that aren't there. And we don't want to violate the time-tested principle: Scripture interprets Scripture. Still reading between the lines is inevitable—and often helpful—as we seek to apply God's truths to our own lives.

Take Asaph's prayer in Psalm 77, for example. We don't know for sure when or why he wrote it. Evidently the words do not flow from the pen of a man lounging beside the motel pool sipping lemonade on vacation. Some great distress has burst into his life, a disaster that robs him of sleep and leaves him feeling helpless. In fact he feels death breathing cold air down his neck.

Then, between the third and fourth paragraphs of Asaph's prayer, something happens. We can't tell from looking at the text how much time elapsed between these paragraphs. Perhaps only seconds. Perhaps weeks or months. But however long the time frame, God has been at work. The Lord has, in grace, entered Asaph's despair and replaced it with hope, with hope in His strength and His saving love. God is great. God does wonders. God shows saving love. God redeems His people:

> What god is great like our God?
> Thou art the God who workest wonders;
> Thou hast made known Thy strength
>   among the peoples.
> Thou hast by Thy power redeemed Thy people.
> (vv. 13–15)

The Lord has reminded Asaph of His Word, His promises of grace, and has through that Word, those promises, created trust in Asaph's heart—trust strong enough and warm enough to evaporate Asaph's fears.

Speak, Lord, Your Servant Is Listening

Does God do the same thing for us when we pray? Does He "talk back" to us, as it were, to remind us of His Word, His love, His promises? Or, is prayer more like slipping our thoughts, our praises, our needs, and our requests under heaven's doormat? Is prayer one-sided, like writing a letter to your governor or e-mailing the White House?

As we begin to answer these questions, we start with this premise: Christian prayer is relational. We *can* pray and we *want* to pray only because Jesus Christ died for us and rose again from the dead. He has become our Brother. God is now our Father. We belong to the family of God; we are heirs of heaven. Our Brother loves us. Our Father loves us. This fact makes Christian prayer quite different than all attempts pagans make to contact their deities. We worship a God who *can* hear us and who *wants* to hear us. We pray to a God who has adopted us into His very own family!

Maybe you know a married couple both of whom live in the same house, but as virtual strangers. He leaves her a note on the refrigerator when he gets up in the morning. She replies with a note on the same refrigerator when she leaves for class late in the afternoon. He jots a note in response just before he goes to bed. She reads it as she races out the door for work the following morning. This is not communication, let alone a family!

In the same way, prayer involves more than leaving a wish list for a god who will try to read it when he gets a spare moment. God wants to spend time with us! What's more, He wants us to know that He is listening when we pray and that He cares—cares deeply—about us and about the things that concern us. This is what He promises:

Call to Me, and I will answer you, and I will tell you great and mighty things, which you do not know. (Jeremiah 33:3)

But what "great and mighty things" does He tell us? And how does He communicate those things? Christians believe God has indeed spoken and that He continues to speak today—in His Word.

God's Word to us is first and foremost "the Word-Made-Flesh"—Jesus Christ (John 1:14). Every time we begin a prayer with the words "Our Father ..." or "Dear Savior ..." or "O most merciful God ...," our Lord's word to us has passed over our lips. We know God as Father because of Jesus. We know God is merciful because of Jesus. We know God as Savior in Jesus. When we say those words (and words like them), the Holy Spirit is already at work through them to strengthen, to reassure, to comfort, and to invite us to open our hearts more fully to receive His grace. These are "great and mighty things" indeed!

Then, perhaps, we turn in our prayers to an acknowledgment of our sins. Suppose we had to do that not already knowing for sure what God's answer would be? Suppose we had to wonder whether this time He might demand we pay our own debt, that we take our own punishment? How frightening! In fact, if that were the case, I dare say none of us could or would ever again approach God's throne. But we do know God's answer to our sin. Before we prodigals start out for home, we know—in Jesus—that our Father will embrace us. Because of the cross—the mighty cross—we have pardon and peace. As we then confess our sins, the Holy Spirit encourages us with the reality of the forgiveness promised in His Word—in Jesus and in the Holy Scriptures. As we continue to pray, God continues to keep the promise Jesus made to us on the night before He died:

> But the Helper, the Holy Spirit, whom the Father will send in My name, He will teach you all things, and bring to your remembrance all that I said to you. (John 14:26)

When the Holy Spirit comes alongside us to help us pray, part of what He does for Christ's people involves reminding us of what our Savior has taught us. With this in mind, it's easy to see the critical link between prayer and the study of Scripture. In fact, we do well to pray with our Bible open all the time! The better we know the Scriptures, the more focused, God-pleasing, and powerful our prayers can be.

Praying God's Word Back to Him

The Bible is the Word and will of God. Therefore when we read a specific command or promise in the Scriptures, we need not wonder whether God wants us to ask Him to fulfill it in us or for us. We can pray in the bold confidence that our request is truly in His will. Take, for instance, the prayers Paul included in his letters to the churches. These inspired prayers express God's changeless will for all His people of every time and place. These are things for which Jesus, our great High Priest, continually intercedes on our behalf. We can pray these prayers for ourselves and for those we love. Here are four of the many prayers Scripture contains:

- *[I pray] ... that the God of our Lord Jesus Christ, the Father of glory, may give to you a spirit of wisdom and of revelation in the knowledge of Him. I pray that the eyes of your heart may be enlightened, so that you may know what is the hope of His calling, what are the riches of the glory of His inheritance in the saints, and what is the surpassing greatness of His power toward us who believe. These are in accordance with the working of the strength of His might which He brought about in Christ, when He raised Him from the dead, and seated Him at His right hand in the heavenly places, far above all rule and authority and power and dominion, and every name that is named, not only in this age, but also in the one to come* (Ephesians 1:17–21).

- *[I pray that God] would grant you, according to the riches of His glory, to be strengthened with power through His Spirit in the inner man; so that Christ may dwell in your hearts through faith; and that you, being rooted and grounded in love, may be able to comprehend with all the saints what is the breadth and length and height and depth, and to know the love of Christ which surpasses knowledge, that you may be filled up to all the fulness of God. Now to Him who is able to do exceeding abun-*

dantly beyond all that we ask or think, according to the power that works within us, to Him be the glory in the church and in Christ Jesus to all generations forever and ever. Amen (Ephesians 3:16–21).

- And this I pray, that your love may abound still more and more in real knowledge and all discernment, so that you may approve the things that are excellent, in order to be sincere and blameless until the day of Christ; having been filled with the fruit of righteousness which comes through Jesus Christ, to the glory and praise of God (Philippians 1:9–11).

- [We pray] that you may be filled with the knowledge of [God's] will in all spiritual wisdom and understanding, so that you may walk in a manner worthy of the Lord, to please Him in all respects, bearing fruit in every good work and increasing in the knowledge of God; strengthened with all power, according to His glorious might, for the attaining of all steadfastness and patience; joyously giving thanks to the Father, who has qualified us to share in the inheritance of the saints in light. For He delivered us from the domain of darkness, and transferred us to the kingdom of His beloved Son, in whom we have redemption, the forgiveness of sins (Colossians 1:9–14).

Wow! Think about the ways our lives and the lives of others might change if we would pray and keep on praying God to grant the requests in just these four prayers!

We can pray other Scriptures too, listening to what our kind Father says to us in them and asking, in turn, that He would grant those things He has revealed He wants. For example, it's not hard to adapt Jesus' High Priestly Prayer in John 17 so that it fits our situation today. Here are a few verses as an example:

> Father, the hour has come; glorify Thy Son, that the Son may glorify Thee, even as Thou gavest Him authority over all mankind, that to all whom Thou hast given Him, He may give eternal life. … I am no more in the world; and yet they themselves are in the world, and I come to Thee. Holy Father, keep them in Thy name, the name which Thou hast given Me, that they may be one, even as We are. While I was with them, I was keeping them in Thy name which Thou hast given Me; and I guarded them, and not one of them perished but the son of perdition, that the Scripture might be fulfilled. … I do not ask Thee to take them out of the world, but to keep them from the evil one. … Sanctify them in the truth; Thy word is truth. (vv. 1–2, 11–12, 15, 17)

Almost any part of the New Testament (and much of the Old Testament as well) can be adapted in this same way so that our prayer time becomes a time of dialog. God speaks to us through His Word. We respond in praise, in worship, in confession, in petition. Then, through His Word, our Lord assures us that we have from Him what we have asked. The Scriptures shape us, and we in turn pray prayers forged by the Scriptures on which we have meditated.

This process is part of what David meant in Psalm 37 when he wrote:

> Delight yourself in the LORD;
> And He will give you the desires of your heart. (v. 4)

God wants to use His Word to fill our hearts with a hunger and thirst for what He wants to give us. All our godly desires come from Him. Then, as we bring those God-given desires before His throne of grace, He gladly fulfills them. Think of the flood of blessings this opens up as you read just a few of God's promises to you:

> Therefore, my beloved brethren, be steadfast, immovable, always abounding in the work of the Lord, knowing that your toil is not in vain in the Lord. (1 Corinthians 15:58)

> For I am confident of this very thing, that He who began a good work in you will perfect it until the day of Christ Jesus. (Philippians 1:6)

> It is God who is at work in you, both to will and to work for His good pleasure. (Philippians 2:13)

> And my God shall supply all your needs according to His riches in glory in Christ Jesus. (Philippians 4:19)

> May the Lord cause you to increase and abound in love for one another, and for all men, just as we also do for you; so that He may establish your hearts unblamable in holiness before our God and Father at the coming of our Lord Jesus with all His saints. (1 Thessalonians 3:12–13)

… that the name of our Lord Jesus may be glorified in you, and you in Him, according to the grace of our God and the Lord Jesus Christ. (2 Thessalonians 1:12)

Beloved, now we are children of God, and it has not appeared as yet what we shall be. We know that, when He appears, we shall be like Him, because we shall see Him just as He is. (1 John 3:2)

But What about … ?

The more familiar we become with Scripture, the more promises we will unearth and then be able to use in our prayers. And yet, not every problem we pray has a specific, detailed promise of Scripture attached to it. Even so, the *principles* of God's Word do apply to any situation in which we find ourselves. For instance, suppose you or someone you love has lost a job. Nothing in the Bible will direct a job applicant to Big Blue Chip Industrial Corp. or to Fast Food King. We do know these truths, though, on the authority of Scripture:

- God wants to give His children wisdom, especially when we face difficulties (e.g., Proverbs 2:1–9).
- It's God's general will that His people live quiet, productive lives. For most of us, this includes work of some kind (e.g., Proverbs 6:6–14).
- God cares for His own; He supplies our needs; He is the Source of our livelihood, we ourselves are not (e.g., Matthew 6:25–34; 1 Peter 5:6–7).

- God gave work to Adam and Eve as a blessing. Because of sin, work can become toilsome. But our gracious Lord still wants His children to find joy and satisfaction in their work (e.g., Ecclesiastes 5:18–20).
- Worry is sinful (e.g., Matthew 6:25–34; 1 Timothy 6:6–12).
- When we don't know what path to take, we can seek godly counsel (e.g., Proverbs 11:14; 15:5, 22; 19:20).

Can you see how a Christian could pray prayers based on these principles and then know with 100 percent certainty that the Lord has heard and is already answering? We could ask, for example, for wisdom in looking for work. We could ask that our Lord would provide wise counsel through others during the time of challenge. We could ask God to fulfill His promise to care for us and for our family. We could ask for contentment with the food and clothing He provides and for a thankful and cheerful heart with which to receive them. And we could ask Him in His perfect timing to provide productive work and joy in doing it.

"But," perhaps you say, "I'm not sure I know the Bible that well. I can't dig out principles like that for the situations I want to pray about!" If that's your admission, then your Lord has a glorious adventure in store for you! He Himself wants to be your Teacher, your Tutor! He wants you to know His will. He Himself will sit down with you as you open the Bible and get to know Him and the ways of His kingdom. Remember Jesus' promise:

But the Helper, the Holy Spirit, whom the Father will send in My name, He will teach you all things, and bring to your remembrance all that I said to you. (John 14:26)

A powerful prayer life cannot exist apart from a growing knowledge of God's Word. But you need not stop praying until you know Scripture better! Those who know Jesus, those who have a personal faith relationship with Him, know the heart of God. That heart is a heart of grace. Prayers based in the grace and mercy of God cannot fall too far from the throne of God:

As for you, the anointing which you received from Him abides in you, and you have no need for anyone to teach you; but as His anointing teaches you about all things, and is true and is not a lie, and just as it has taught you, you abide in Him. (1 John 2:27)

A well-worn analogy compares the connection between Scripture meditation and prayer to the process of respiration. We breathe in the atmosphere of heaven as we ponder the truths of God's Word. And we respond to that Word by breathing out prayers of praise, confession, and petition. This process—both parts working together as one—is one of the key indicators of a healthy Christian life.

LOOKING AHEAD

We end where we began. Jesus loves to answer prayer. Jesus equips us to pray. Jesus uses our prayers to advance His kingdom. We are armed and dangerous as we assault the kingdom of darkness for the glory of Christ whenever we pray for ourselves, for our loved ones, and for "the nations"—those who don't yet know Jesus. What an exciting privilege! What an awesome opportunity! As you continue to grow in your prayer life, "May the Lord direct your hearts into the love of God and into the steadfastness of Christ" (2 Thessalonians 3:5).

LOOKING INWARD AND UPWARD

Talk with God about your answers to these questions. Share your insights with your prayer partner or with others in your prayer group. What do you learn?

- What Scriptures do you or would you most like to pray for yourself? Why?
- What Scriptures do you or would you most like to pray for someone else? Explain.
- What has your Teacher, the Holy Spirit, taught you lately about yourself and about your God? How did He do that?
- How could you integrate the Scriptures more thoroughly into your prayer life?

PRACTICAL PRAYER TIP

Individuals and prayer groups often pray extemporaneous prayers in response to God's goodness and people's needs. Such prayers, based on the Word and will of God, please Him. More formal prayers like those found in hymnals or prayer books often include phrases or whole verses of Scripture. These prayers also express

God's goodness and our human need. Based on the Word and will of God, they please Him. If you most often pray extemporaneous prayers, try praying a few formal prayers during your prayer time too. If you usually pray from a prayer book, add some extemporaneous prayers to your routine. In either case, you may well find yourself stretched and growing as your prayer life is enriched. See Appendix D.

APPENDIX A

Teaching Kids to Pray

When did you first learn to pray? Did Dad teach you? Or Grandma? Did you learn as your family prayed a blessing on your food before you ate each meal? Or, did you first cry out to God for help as you lay face in the dirt during a firefight in Vietnam? Or on a hospital bed the night before cancer surgery?

However you first learned to pray, the fact that you're reading this book says that prayer is something important to you. Perhaps you picked it up because you wanted to broaden your understanding or because you wonder about prayer's effectiveness or because you wanted to find ways to pray more consistently. In any case, your interest in prayer and the blessings God gives us in prayer may move you to want to teach someone else—perhaps a child or grandchild—to pray. How can you do that?

1. First, pray for wisdom for yourself. Pray also that our Lord would plant the desire to pray in the heart and mind of the child. Then trust God to do that. (Compare 1 Chronicles 22:12 with 2 Chronicles 1:7–10; Solomon's desire for godly wisdom was no accident!)

2. Model prayer. Let your child see and hear you pray. Show prayer's importance by praying.

3. Involve your child in prayer—at whatever age. Even 3- and 4-year-olds can repeat simple words and brief phrases after you. Or pray "finish it" prayers together. You pray, "Dear Jesus, thank You for _____," and let your child fill in the blank.

4. Choose one meal prayer and pray it consistently until your child can join in the words. Then learn a second prayer. After you've learned three or four, let your child choose which one to pray. (See pages 160–61 for examples.)

5. Make prayer time part of your bedtime ritual. Have your child suggest prayer thoughts by asking questions like

   • *What happy times can we thank Jesus for giving us today?*

- *Who is sick or afraid? Let's ask Jesus to help them.*
- *What else would you like to say to Jesus?*

6. When your child gets older, take turns praying. Finish sentences like those below yourself. Then pause while your child does the same.

   - *Dear Jesus, You're so great. I praise You for …*
   - *Dear Jesus, I sinned today. Please forgive me for …*
   - *Dear Jesus, thank You for …*
   - *Dear Jesus, please help …*

7. Keep prayer time brief and positive. If your child has nothing to say to Jesus on a given night or doesn't want to pray aloud, don't force him or her. Simply pray yourself and let it go at that.

8. As your child grows and learns to read with more skill, provide prayer books. Decide together on a prayer or two to read on a given night in addition to your extemporaneous prayers.

9. Talk to Jesus at times other than bedtime or mealtime too. Ask for His protection before you set out on vacation or on icy roads. Thank Him for His goodness as you unpack the groceries. Pray for people who are hurt or in danger when you hear sirens. Make talking to Jesus as comfortable and natural as conversing with your best friends.

10. Keep praying for your child's spiritual life as you go along. Be sure your child overhears some of

these prayers. Your love will make a difference and Jesus' love will make even more of a difference in your child's life.

APPENDIX B

A Personal Prayer Retreat

Have you ever thought about setting aside some time to get alone with your Lord? Christians who practice the habit of taking personal retreats find it helpful and spiritually refreshing. Here are some general ideas about personal retreats some of God's people have found helpful. Choose from among them those you think would be most workable for you. Take the suggestions you think best and leave the rest for use at another time.

- Get away from your usual surroundings; do this even if you live alone. A change of scene most often results in a change of mind-set. Sometimes

I check into an inexpensive motel. Other times, I simply camp out in my guest bedroom. For a short retreat—say, a half-day—I pack my Bible and a notebook and head for a park near my home. Pick a place and an extended period of time in which you can be reached in an emergency, but where there's a good chance you will not be disturbed—either by another person or by the dirty laundry calling to you from the hamper.

- Some couples covenant to cover for each other within the family, trading off retreat weekends. He agrees to take care of the kids and household responsibilities one Saturday every three months, and she covers those same responsibilities so he can get away the following weekend. Time with Jesus is a great gift husbands and wives can offer each other!

- Set aside as long a time period as you can. I find myself getting the most out of two or even three days. But don't think of the possibilities as "all or nothing." If you can only squeeze four hours out of your calendar this quarter, take it. It's four hours more than you will have if you don't! Decide ahead of time to leave the television and radio off. Forego newspapers and magazines too. If you're a television junkie or if you're used to lots of noise and activity, expect the first several hours to feel somewhat uncomfortable. Our culture has found ways to scream messages (most of them commercial) at us during almost every waking second. Stepping out of this stream can be disorienting, especially at first. But as you settle into the quiet, you will probably find it relaxing.

- Take only a few, carefully selected tools with you:
  ❏ Your Bible, of course.

  ❏ Perhaps a hymnal or another devotional book you find helpful.

  ❏ A notebook and some pens or pencils.

  ❏ Possibly a concordance or topical word book (such as Nave's).

  ❏ An audiocassette tape or CD with hymns, Scripture songs, or praise choruses.

  ❏ An audiocassette tape player or CD player.

- I usually pack my favorite mug, some tea bags or instant cocoa, and one of those electric warmers that hangs on the inside of the cup and boils water in two minutes flat. (You may want to take along change for the soda machine if you prefer cold drinks.)

- Most important, ask your Lord to prepare your heart to meet with Him. Ask that He protect you from spiritual pride and from undue personal introspection. Our goal is to focus on our Savior. Our goal is to glorify, to honor, and to learn from Him, not to prove to ourselves or to anyone else how "superspiritual" we are. Ask that He guide you through the retreat process toward those goals and that He transform you more fully into His image (Romans 12:1–2).

- Have in mind a general plan for your time, but be willing to deviate from that plan if the Lord seems to take you in another direction. Be sure, though, that your direction comes from His Word.
- Decide ahead of time, with God's help, to steer a clear course between two extremes—day-dreaming and catnapping all your time away on the one hand, and cramming as though for a seminary final exam on the other. Think of your retreat with Jesus as just that, a time to retreat from the obligations and clutter of everyday life for the express purpose of getting to know your best Friend just a little better. Balance study with reflection and reflection with relaxation and relaxation with prayer.

Personal Prayer Retreat 1—A Focus on Praise (4–6 hours)

Choose three or four of the activities from the list below. All of them focus on prayers of praise. As you go along, ask your Lord to deepen your appreciation of Him and your awe at His majesty and grace. Also ask that this awe and appreciation would carry over into those times you praise Him with other believers, especially in public worship with your congregation each week. Note that most of the activities can be repeated several times.

- Review chapter 2, *The Sacrifice of Praise*.
- Think about the questions on pp. 24–25 and write your responses in your notebook. Take

your time. The first question, in particular, has more than one answer. As you think of implications, write as many as you can. Work toward getting five—or 10, or even 20!

- Revelation 19:1–6 describes the worship service that is taking place in heaven right now. What elements of that service would you like God to import into your worship here on earth? Why? What would you like to say to Him about that? Write your prayer in the form of a letter.

- Meditate on God's attributes, those characteristics He has revealed about Himself in the Scriptures (e.g., the fact that He is faithful, gracious, all-powerful).

  ❏ List these attributes as you think of them. How many could you name?

  ❏ Now look through the Scriptures, particularly Paul's letters in the New Testament (Romans through Philemon). Add as many more attributes to your list as you can find.

  ❏ Now think again about each entry on your list. Jot a few notes next to each to remind yourself of why you personally are glad God is *gracious* or *just* or *forgiving*.

  ❏ Use your list as the basis of a prayer of praise. Talk to your Savior-God about what He's like and about what that means to you.

  ❏ Page through the book of Psalms, particularly Psalms 90–150. Find two or three that you would characterize as mostly or completely praise psalms (rather than psalms of thanks or of petition). Focus on these prayers of praise one at a time. Remember that the Holy Spirit inspired the psalmist to compose each psalm and to record each for our instruction and use. As you study and as you pray each psalm back to God, think about the details it gives and about how each detail expands your picture of your Lord.

❑ How does this, in turn, lift your heart to your Savior-God in praise? Jot notes to yourself, either in your Bible or your notebook.

❑ Then talk to God about the thoughts, questions, and feelings this exercise raised for you.

Personal Prayer Retreat 2—A Focus on the Kingdom of Christ (1 or 2 days)

As you plan for this one- or two-day retreat, you may want to gather several issues of your congregation's monthly newsletter, informational brochures from one or two Christian outreach organizations or mission fields that you most care about, and perhaps a newspaper or magazine that reports national and international news. You will also need the items listed on p. 139.

Create your own activities. Or, choose from among the activities suggested below those that strike you as most stimulating or growth-provoking. If you begin an exercise that seems to go nowhere at first, ask the Lord for guidance and insight. Then spend 10 additional minutes on it. If the exercise still goes nowhere, set it aside for another time and move on to the next activity. Perhaps you will return to it later in this retreat. Or maybe weeks or months from now, you'll find yourself drawn to finish it. Remember, God's Spirit must lead us into His Word; we can't force ourselves there. He knows best how to nourish His people.

Look over the activities before you start out. Be sure to take along any additional materials or supplies you will want to use as you complete them.

- Review chapter 5, *Thy Kingdom Come!* Underline as you skim it. What thoughts or ideas come to mind as you personalize the concepts there?

- Respond to some or all of the questions at the end of that chapter (pp. 60–61). Record those responses in your notebook. How do you react as you think about yourself having an ongoing part to play in bringing Christ's kingdom to "the nations" as you pray for that to happen?

- Find the "missions" or "society" section in your hymnal or prayer book. Pray some of these hymns or prayers.

  ❏ Choose a favorite hymn or prayer from the book. Imagine you could interview the writer. What would you expect that person's heart to be like? Describe it as fully as you can in your notebook.

  ❏ Analyze Acts 13:1–5, the account of the church in Antioch sending Paul and Barnabas out on the first missionary journey. What kind of heart had God given the senders? What kind of heart had He given those who were sent? Describe your thoughts as fully as you can after you've read the text three or four times.

❑ Now think about the fact that you stand right now in the presence of **the** "spiritual heart surgeon." Ask the Holy Spirit to examine your own heart and reveal to you any attitudes that get in the way of your praying for "the nations"—those people and groups worldwide who don't know Christ Jesus as Savior and Lord. Confess any sins you see. Ask for His forgiveness and healing. Ask that He open your eyes to see the world as He sees it and that He give you a burden for the lost.

❑ Write a poem or hymn yourself to express God's heart of love for those who don't know Him. You may want to use Scripture verses as a starting point, for instance parts of John 10 or Isaiah 55:1–7.

• Take a walk. Ask Jesus to walk with you. As you walk, talk to Him about your walk through life to this point and about the lives your life has touched along the way. Focus in particular on those lives you are touching right now.

❑ How are you an ambassador of Christ's kingdom for each of these people?

❑ How could you more fully and accurately represent Him and His kingdom?

❑ Pray about this, but remember that the power to live as Jesus' representative comes only from Him, not from our trying hard to do it.

❑ Copy the words of 2 Corinthians 3:5 or 4:7 on a small piece of paper or on a note card. Read it several dozen times throughout this retreat as you meditate on its meaning. Memorize it if you can, as you ask your Lord to make this truth more real for you.

- Read your congregational newsletters or the mission field brochures you brought along. As you do that, look for needs, challenges, and people you could pray about. List these.

  ❑ Now break the list down into seven days of prayer lists, two or three items on each day's list. Plan to use these lists in the days and weeks ahead. Ask yourself, "What can I ask God to do for and through my congregation (or this mission organization)? What can I ask God to do for and through *me* as I support these organizations, people, and activities?"

  ❑ Write one or more letters of thanks and encouragement to those in charge of the activities or organizations for which you are praying. Assure them of your prayers. If you are open to it, offer to intercede for specific needs they may have.

❑ Take time to pray through all seven lists at least once during this time of retreat. Ask that God would give you His heart for the kingdom work about which you are praying.

- The book of Matthew stresses the coming of Christ's kingdom. Read it in one sitting. (This will take an hour or two if you read straight through.) As you read, look for evidence of the kingdom's coming, its citizens, and its characteristics. Jot notes to yourself about passages to which you want to return so you can study them in more depth.

  ❑ What conclusions can you draw about the kingdom of Christ?

  ❑ What implications do you see for praying "Thy kingdom come"?

- Use a blank sheet of paper and some marking pens to make a "name collage." Include on this collage the names of individuals or families whom you know personally that were once in God's family, but who have dropped by the wayside for one reason or another. Include people close to you, people at work, people in your family, people in your neighborhood, and also people about whom you know very little else, other than their lapse in faith. Think of children and teens as well as adults. Intercede for these people, by name. Ask that the Lord find a way to bring them back to Himself, to grant whatever repentance is needed, and to show you if He would involve you in any way to accomplish this.

- Study Psalm 2, line by line. You might try copying it in the center of a large piece of white paper. Leave wide margins. Then use another color of ink to write notes to yourself in the margins. If your Bible has cross-references, look them up.

  ❏ What new insights about the coming of God's kingdom do you gain?

  ❏ Copy the words of Matthew 28:18–20 at the bottom of the page. What connections do you see between Psalm 2 and the Great Commission?

  ❏ Keep these two Scriptures in mind as you use colored pencils to color a copy of the world map on pp.148–149. Pray for each nation or continent as you do this. You may find it helpful to play hymns or Scripture songs on your CD player as you work. Let your heart join the heart of Jesus as together you intercede for the nations.

- Think about the part you have been playing in the coming of Christ's kingdom.

  ❏ Are you *fully satisfied, partly satisfied, partly dissatisfied,* or *totally dissatisfied* as you think about that role? In your notebook, explain why you answered as you did.

Lord, Give U

he Nations!

❑ Talk to God about it. Include your frustrations or fears, your joys and His grace, and any challenges or roadblocks you face. Say anything you need to say. Remember that Jesus is your "Wonderful Counselor" (Isaiah 9:6).

• Before you prepare to return home, allow about 30 minutes to pray the Lord's Prayer. As you pray each phrase out loud, think about the needs of the world and of your community for the Gospel. Elaborate on the prayer as you pray it. For example:

Our Father ... thank You that You have made me a part of Your family, kind Father. Yet, I know that there are so many who do not see You in that light, who do not know You through Your Son, Jesus. Father, help me to love them as You Yourself love them. ... **Who art in heaven** ... You made the world and all that exists. You have the power to do whatever You please. And you have been pleased to send Jesus to die on the cross for me and for all people. Look down from heaven on the world You so love and have mercy on those who are lost and wandering far from home ...

A week or two after your retreat ends, take a few moments to look back over what you did during that time. Follow up on any ideas that still seem to have merit. Jot down any ideas you have for the next retreat you take. Above all, review the grace of God that is always yours in Christ and the ways He revealed that to you in His Word during the time you spent with Him.

APPENDIX C

A Prayer Retreat for Groups

If you plan a retreat for your church's prayer group, you may want to use *Armed and Dangerous: Praying with Boldness* as a resource. For a weekend retreat, focus on these chapters:

1. Armed and Dangerous (Introduction)

2. The Sacrifice of Praise (Praise)

3. Coals from Heaven's High Altar (Confession)

5. Thy Kingdom Come! (Praying for the Lost)

6. Praying in the Will of God (Praying for Health, Family Problems, Finances)

9. Prayer Is Not a Prelude (Prayer and Serving God)

Here is one sample schedule:

Friday Evening

7:00   Welcome and Opening Worship
       (Whole group)

7:30   Armed and Dangerous
       (Large and small group)

8:30   Recreation and Relaxation
       (Whole group)

Saturday Morning

8:30   Breakfast

9:00   Opening Worship
       (Whole group)

9:15   The Sacrifice of Praise
       (Large and small group)

10:00 A Time of Praise
       (Whole group)

10:30 Break

11:00 Coals from Heaven's High Altar
       (Large and small group)

12:00 Lunch

1:00   Thy Kingdom Come!
       (Large and small group)

2:15	A Prayer Walk
	(Individual)
3:00	Thy Will Be Done
	(Large and small group)
4:00	Prayer
	(Prayer Partners)
5:00	Dinner
6:00	Worship video or film
	(Whole group)
6:45	Recreation and relaxation

Sunday Morning

8:00	Individual Prayer Time
8:30	Breakfast
9:30	Prayer Is Not a Prelude
	(Large and small group)
10:30	A Service of Prayer and Worship
11:30	Dismissal

From this bare-bones skeleton you can create a retreat that fits your setting and your group. Here are some further ideas and explanations based on the schedule above:

- Choose a setting away from your church building if you can. A camp or retreat center with a chapel would be ideal.
- The presenter can share the ideas and concepts from each individual chapter listed in the

schedule. This should take about 20–30 minutes for each topic. Then have participants form groups of 4–6 each. Display some or all of the questions and activities from the end of the chapter, "Looking Inward, Looking Upward," on large sheets of poster paper, on an overhead projector, or on large individual note cards—one card for each small group. When 5–10 minutes remain in each session, call for the group's attention and share ideas, questions, and insights with one another.

- Distribute copies of *Armed and Dangerous* as the retreat ends. Point out Appendix F and suggest that participants duplicate the seven pages of prayer list paper there to use as directed on page 169.

- The schedule above suggests a "worship video" for use on Saturday evening. The film distributor your congregation uses should be able to help you find a suitable piece. Many Christian film companies have produced music videos that feature nature scenes and orchestrated hymns to accompany the visuals. The effect, in many cases, is quite beautiful and worshipful. You'll want to darken the room for best effect.

- Plan a way to provide music for group worship. Live worship leaders with appropriate instruments would be ideal. But if necessary, you can use prerecorded music. If you take this route, provide the best quality CD player and speakers possible. The person in charge of playing this music should *practice* with the equipment ahead of time so as to make smooth transitions between selections. Give participants song sheets or display lyrics on an overhead projector. Take care to obtain appropriate permission to use copyrighted songs and hymns.

- The **Prayer Walk** suggested for Saturday at 2:15 could be repeated as an option at 9:00 on Sunday morning. It will work best if your group meets in a setting where it's possible to walk outdoors. Simply have participants spend time in private prayer as they walk around the grounds of the retreat center. Or, see Appendix B for more detailed directions about a prayer walk that's closely tied to the prayer "Thy Kingdom Come."

- Encourage participants to choose a prayer partner for the retreat and provide times and places for partners to pray together, perhaps in the chapel. Draw names, let people select a partner on their own, or come up with a more creative way to match people with one another (e.g., pairs of matching breakfast placemats).

- If possible, have your pastor lead the Sunday morning time of worship. Ask him to encourage participants in their role as intercessors for the congregation and for the church at large. If a pastor is not available, use this block of time as a prayer service. Allow time for each kind of prayer you have studied—praise, confession, and intercession for the kingdom of Christ and for individuals both in and outside His kingdom of grace. Psalms 149, 32, 2, and 34 would be appropriate Scriptures to include in this time of prayer.

- Schedule a one-Sunday, follow-up Bible study a week or two after the retreat based on chapter 10, "Hearing God Speak When We Pray." Allow time for participants to share questions and experiences that have come up since the retreat. Serve refreshments and use the time to encourage participants to continue the prayer partnerships they began during your weekend together.

APPENDIX D

Prayers Other Believers Have Prayed

Luther's Morning Prayer

I thank You, my heavenly Father, through Jesus Christ, Your dear Son, that You have kept me this night from all harm and danger; and I pray that You would keep me this day also from sin and every evil, that all my doings and life may please You. For into Your hands I commend myself, my body and soul, and all things. Let Your holy angel be with me, that the evil foe may have no power over me. Amen.

LUTHER'S EVENING PRAYER

I thank You, my heavenly Father, through Jesus Christ, Your dear Son, that You have graciously kept me this day; and I pray that You would forgive me all my sins where I have done wrong, and graciously keep me this night. For into Your hands I commend myself, my body and soul, and all things. Let Your holy angel be with me, that the evil foe may have no power over me. Amen.

FOR THE CHURCH

Merciful God, we humbly implore You to cast the bright beams of Your light upon Your Church that we, being instructed by the doctrine of the blessed apostles, may walk in the light of Your truth and at length attain to the light of everlasting life; through Jesus Christ, our Lord. Amen.

FOR THE RIGHT WORSHIP OF GOD

Heavenly Father, God of all grace, waken our hearts that we may never forget your blessings but steadfastly thank and praise You for all Your goodness, that we may live in Your fear until with all Your saints we praise You eternally in Your heavenly kingdom; through Jesus Christ, our Lord. Amen.

FOR DIVINE PROTECTION

O God, because You justify the ungodly and desire not the death of the sinner, we humbly implore You graciously to assist by Your heavenly aid, and evermore shield with Your divine protection, Your servants who trust in Your mercy, that they may be separated from You by no temptations but may serve You without ceasing; through Jesus Christ, our Lord. Amen.

For Likeness to Christ

O God, by the patient suffering of Your only-begotten Son You have beaten down the pride of the old enemy. Now help us, we humbly pray, rightly to treasure in our hearts all that our Lord has of His goodness borne for our sake that after His example we may bear with patience all that is adverse to us; through Jesus Christ, our Lord. Amen.

Before Worship

O Lord, our Creator, Redeemer, and Comforter, as we come together to worship You in spirit and in truth, we humbly pray that You may open our hearts to the preaching of Your Word, so that we may repent of our sins, believe in Jesus Christ as our only Savior, and grow in grace and holiness. Hear us for His sake. Amen.

After Worship

Almighty and merciful God, we have again worshiped in Your presence and have received forgiveness for our many sins and the assurance of Your love in Jesus Christ. We thank You for this undeserved grace and ask

You to keep us in faith until we inherit eternal salvation; through Jesus Christ, our Lord. Amen.

FOR PEACE

O God, from whom all holy desires, all good counsels, and all just works proceed, give to Your servants that peace which the world cannot give that our hearts may be set to obey Your commandments and also that we, being defended by You, may pass our time in rest and quietness; through the merits of Jesus Christ, our Savior. Amen.

FOR MISSIONARY WORK

Almighty God, since you have called Your Church to witness that in Christ You have reconciled us to Yourself, grant that by Your Holy Spirit we may proclaim the good news of Your salvation that all who hear it may receive the gift of salvation; through Jesus Christ, our Lord. Amen.

CHILDREN'S MEALTIME PRAYERS

Come, Lord Jesus, be our Guest, and let Your gifts to us be blessed. Amen.

⊶⊷

God is great, God is good; and we thank Him for our food. Amen.

⊶⊷

Bless this food, dear Lord, we pray. Make us thankful every day. Amen.

Our hands we fold, our heads we bow; for food and drink we thank Thee now. Amen.

Oh, give thanks unto the Lord, for He is good; for His mercy endures forever. Amen.

Thank You for the world so sweet. Thank You for the food we eat. Thank You for the birds that sing. Thank You, God, for everything. Amen.

CHILDREN'S BEDTIME PRAYERS

Bless everyone I love, God. And bless me too. Amen.

Now I lay me down to sleep. I pray You, Lord, Your child to keep. Send happy dreams and near me stay until another happy day. Amen.

Jesus, tender Shepherd, hear me. Bless Your little child tonight. Through the darkness, please be near me. Keep me safe till morning's light. Amen.

The day is done; O God the Son, look down upon Your little one!

O God of Light, keep me this night, and send to me Your angels bright. I need not fear if You are near; You are my Savior, kind and dear. Amen.

APPENDIX E

For Prayer Groups Only

Whether you pray once each month with a group of people from your church or once each day on the telephone with one prayer partner, your Lord wants to encourage and strengthen you in the intercessory work He has given you the privilege of undertaking. Four specific temptations can derail that holy work. Ask His grace to guard your heart against them in these four ways:

FOCUS ON JESUS

He is the Savior. He is the Healer. He is the Prince of Peace. He is the Wonderful Counselor. He is the Giver of all good things. A focus on Him as the answer to all the needs for which we pray and as the only Source of help in the lives of those for whom we pray will protect us from spiritual pride.

Satan wants to trip us up or at least slow us down by encouraging us to think that our prayers make us "better Christians" or "more spiritual" people than other believers we know. If he can skew our vision just slightly, he can get us to believe that because we spend so much time or energy praying, God owes us an answer. Or, he can trick us into thinking that our prayers will twist God's arm or that other people ought to be grateful that we intercede for them. Such misbeliefs rob us of the joy God wants us to have as we pray for others. And it robs God of the glory that rightly belongs to Him when He meets the needs in the lives of those for whom we pray.

Ask the Holy Spirit to help you focus on Jesus and not on yourself when you pray.

HONOR CONFIDENTIALITY

When the people around you learn that you pray for others, they will sometimes bring their own prayer requests to you. I've had virtual strangers in parks and fast-food restaurants share some of the most intimate pain of their lives with me—an impending divorce, gambling debts, adultery, joblessness, a son or daughter on drugs. They have shared names, dates, and specific facts—the kind of grist that could keep a gossip mill grinding for decades. People may sometimes share these kinds of personal details with you too.

Respect the fact that when people do this, they see you not so much as the individual you are but, instead, as a representative of Christ Himself. Treat the information they share as totally confidential unless they tell you otherwise. If someone shares a plan to hurt himself or someone else, you need to take action to prevent it. But in all other cases, you may talk about what you have heard with God alone.

Ask the Holy Spirit to help you honor the confidentiality of the information people share with you.

LET GOD CARRY THE LOAD

As we saw in chapter 8, discouragement can set in when prayer groups work through the same lists of needs month by month. It can seem at times that our Lord is not listening. When we begin to feel that way, we need to remember that He asks *us* to pray, but He reserves for *Himself* the decisions about the most helpful time and methods by which to grant our requests.

We need to help one another fight the temptation to discouragement. That's one reason prayer groups or a prayer partner can be so helpful. When we find ourselves disheartened, wondering, or even worried, others in the group can remind us of God's promises and of His love for us and for those we're praying for. Then when our prayer-partners find themselves disillusioned, we can do the same for them. We need one another in the body of Christ, especially as we serve Him by interceding for others.

Ask the Holy Spirit to protect you from discouragement and to help everyone with whom you pray to praise Him for the work He does, even when you don't see that work at the time.

Pray More, Chat Less

Most of God's people enjoy being together with other believers. We want to support one another and to share one another's joys and sorrows. When we meet with other intercessors, we want to update one another on the situations for which we are interceding. All this can be part of the blessing of belonging to a prayer group.

Quite often, though, prayer groups can wake up at the end of the evening to find they have chatted with one another for 90 minutes and prayed for only 15. No one intends that this happen, it just does. And once in awhile no harm really comes of it. But if talking with one another regularly replaces talking with Jesus, the group won't live up to its high calling. Best case, it will become a social group; on the darker side, it can become an arena for gossip and troublemaking in the congregation.

You may want to appoint a prayer group leader, or you may want to trade leadership duties from meeting to meeting. The leader then holds the group accountable for getting down to prayer after a brief time for socializing. Plan to share light refreshments and fellowship after your prayer time together. Taken together, prayer and fellowship build trust among group members, a trust that is necessary if your group is to enjoy fully the blessings our Lord Jesus gave to the early church:

> And the congregation of those who believed were of one heart and soul; and not one of them claimed that anything belonging to him was his own; but all things were common property to them. (Acts 4:32)

That's the kind of love the Lord Jesus wants all His people to share. It's the beautiful kind of fellowship He wants the people in your prayer group to enjoy. Ask the Holy Spirit to build this kind of Christian love within your group. Ask too that He help you set proper priorities as you get together to intercede for those outside your group.

APPENDIX F

A Personal Prayer Journal

The pages that follow this one include primarily space for you to record notes about your own prayers. Feel free to duplicate them as often as you like for your own personal use. You may want to compile new prayer journal entries every week and/or new prayer lists each month or quarter. We have sized the pages to fit many 6-ring daily organizer systems. If you do not already own a notebook this size, you will be able to purchase one at almost any discount department store or office supply store. Or, simply staple the pages together. Most copy machines will be able to enlarge the pages or to shrink them further if you think another page size will work better for you.

EVERY DAY

○

○

○

○

○

○

The eyes of the LORD are toward the righteous,
And His ears are open to their cry (Psalm 34:15).

MONDAY

Call upon Me in the day of trouble; I shall rescue you, and you will honor Me (Psalm 50:15).

TUESDAY

○

_____

○ _____

_____

○ _____

_____

_____

_____

_____

_____

_____

_____

○ _____

_____

○ _____

_____

○ *For Thou, Lord, art good, and ready to forgive,*
And abundant in lovingkindness to all who call
upon Thee (Psalm 86:5).

WEDNESDAY

*[God says,] "It will also come to pass
that before they call, I will answer;
and while they are still speaking,
I will hear" (Isaiah 65:24).*

THURSDAY

....

○

_____

○

_____

_____

○

_____

_____

_____

_____

_____

_____

_____

○

_____

_____

○

_____

_____

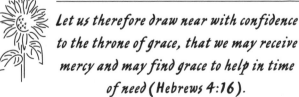

○

Let us therefore draw near with confidence
to the throne of grace, that we may receive
mercy and may find grace to help in time
of need (Hebrews 4:16).

FRIDAY

○

○

○

○

○

○

This is the confidence which we have before Him, that, if we ask anything according to His will, He hears us (1 John 5:14–15).

Saturday/Sunday

*In the same way the Spirit also helps our weakness;
for we do not know how to pray as we should,
but the Spirit Himself intercedes for us with
groanings too deep for words (Romans 8:26).*